A  WORLD  ELSEWHERE

# A World Elsewhere

## THE PLACE OF STYLE
## IN AMERICAN LITERATURE

## RICHARD POIRIER

OXFORD UNIVERSITY PRESS

LONDON    OXFORD    NEW YORK

OXFORD UNIVERSITY PRESS

London   Oxford   New York
Glasgow   Toronto   Melbourne   Wellington
Cape Town   Ibadan   Nairobi   Dar es Salaam   Lusaka   Addis Ababa
Delhi   Bombay   Calcutta   Madras   Karachi   Lahore   Dacca
Kuala Lumpur   Singapore   Hong Kong   Tokyo

To Jean Morton and Philip Poirier

# Preface

What manner of building shall we build?
. . .
In this house, what manner of utterance shall there be?
                Wallace Stevens, "Architecture,"
                        *Opus Posthumous*

We have built for this world a family mansion, and for the next a family tomb. The best works of art are the expression of man's struggle to free himself from this condition, but the effect of our art is merely to make this low state comfortable and that higher state to be forgotten.                THOREAU, "Economy," *Walden*


That the New World offered architectural opportunities on a scale never equaled before or since scarcely needs repeating, any more than does the explanation that American writers have therefore been addicted to metaphors of "building" and to theories about the proper housing for expanded states of consciousness. In Emerson and his successors, including Stevens, "building" refers less to structures in the world, however, than to structures of the mind and to analogous structures of language. The instances in American literature of this kind of "building" are an index to something more important than the recurrence of images, metaphors, or aesthetic theories. My emphasis in this book will be on the dialectical struggle which this concept has engendered within American writing from Emerson and Cooper to the present.

As a conscious play of ideas within works or among

writers, this struggle is almost platitudinously obvious and usually defined as part of the fight for literary as well as political independence of Europe. I have tried instead to locate the phenonemon in style, in the rhythms and sounds of sentences, where it has an energy the more intense because of the writer's usually unprogrammatic involvement with the only materials— language — with which he can try to "build" a world. As it is used in this book, the word style refers to grammar, syntax, and tropes only by way of defining some more significant aspect of style: the sounds, identities, and presences shaped by these technical aspects of expression. Style, as the saying goes, is the man, though in American literature that man is thereby often given a grotesque variety of shapes even within a sentence or a paragraph.

Any such inquiry is of necessity illustrative, detailed, and therefore selective. The direction and proportions of the book did not allow me to give as much attention to some writers, especially to Poe and Melville, as I should like to have given, and I am often guilty, intentionally, of choosing passages from other writers that are notoriously familiar, perhaps by now even tiresome. By choosing well-known works and passages I mean to show that even where familiarity has made readers most at home with American literature there exists unrecognized, within the language, very discomforting agitations of style. One way or another, the marvelous and eccentric vitality of American writing (and one often feels of American life) has been pacified or explicated away by commentators. By being historical about American literature we have often missed the history which is particular novels, poems, or essays, the history lurking in their stylistic and formal characteristics. This is a deprivation not rectified by more recent efforts to extract history from these works in assemblages of images and archtypes.

That writing exists not to be clarified but as a kind of drama of the search for clarity, that symbols, myths, and summaries are themselves only stabs in the dark, are among the presuppositions of this book. The great works of American literature are alive with the effort to stabilize certain feelings and attitudes that have, as it were, no place in the world, no place at all except where a writer's style can give them one. And the attempt to do so occurs, especially in works of the last century, within the context of inhospitable styles and structures. Language is never "free"; its forms are never "new," and it is slightly unfaithful to those who proclaim the possibilities of "freedom" or "newness."

American literature is a struggle with already existing literary, social, and historical organizations for power over environment and over language itself, and it is possible to describe this struggle only by first giving critically evaluative attention to a writer's performance. My own attempts at criticism, especially of Emerson and Mark Twain, are in the interest, then, not of displacement but of an increased appreciation for the difficulties in which they found themselves as writers.

The effort to create a world in which consciousness might be free to explore its powers and affinities has in America been a largely prosaic rather than a poetic enterprise. It has been an attempt, exemplified in some of Thoreau's puns, to include the ordinary sense of the world and the word in an expanded, seamless Reality.

The style of the most exciting American books is not one of consensus or amelioration among its given constituents, but a style filled with an agitated desire to make a world in which tensions and polarities are fully developed and then resolved. The struggle exists throughout American literature, and shows even less respect for chronology than I have.

I want to thank my students at Rutgers and at Harvard who helped me understand some of the issues in this book and Miss Elizabeth Durkee for her cheerful patience and intelligence while I was preparing the manuscript. Martin Duberman, William Taylor, and my brother Philip Poirier have given advice which forces me to admire historians much more than I once thought I should, and I am greatly indebted to Leo Bersani for his conversations and writings about French and American literature. Paul Bertram and William Abrahams have saved me from errors, confusions, and bad taste; Sheldon Meyer at Oxford Press has at all times encouraged me with his generosity and understanding. To Maureen Howard, Dan Howard, to William Phillips and to Robert Hill I am greatly indebted for kindness, good company, and help while I was finishing this work.

During the writing I received generous financial assistance from the Bollingen Foundation and from the Research Council at Rutgers. Chapter Four is an enlarged and considerably revised version of an essay first printed in *In Defense of Reading,* a collection which I had the privilege of editing with Reuben Brower. It is reprinted here with permission of the publishers E. P. Dutton. Part of Chapter Five dealing with Edith Wharton is an expanded version of an essay published in *The*

*American Novel,* edited by Wallace Stegner, and re-printed here with permission of Basic Books.

*New Brunswick, New Jersey*
*June 1966.*

# Contents

# A WORLD ELSEWHERE

# I

## Self and Environment

The most interesting American books are an image of
the creation of America itself, of the effort, in the words
of Emerson's Orphic poet, to "Build therefore your own
world." American writers who make this effort are, in
one sense, only doing what writers, especially in the romantic tradition, have always done. To "enclose" the
world, as Emerson puts it, so that "Time and space, lib-
erty and necessity, are left at large no longer," is to do
no more in Concord than had already been done in
Coleridge's lime tree bower. But such images have a recognizable uniqueness when they occur in American
books. They are bathed in the myths of American history; they carry the metaphoric burden of a great dream
of freedom — of the expansion of national consciousness
into the vast spaces of a continent and the absorption of
those spaces into ourselves. Expansive characters in
Cooper or Emerson, Melville, James, or Fitzgerald are
thus convinced as if by history of the practical possibility of enclosing the world in their imaginations. It is as
if the conventions of English romantic poetry could in
America take on the life of prose, assume a reality that

even history might recognize and that novels could report as news. Let us for the moment assume with Hegel that "freedom" is a creation not of political institutions but of consciousness, that freedom is that reality which the consciousness creates for itself. The assumption makes it more understandable that the creation of America out of a continental vastness is to some degree synonymous in the imagination with the creation of freedom, of an open space made free, once savagery has been dislodged, for some unexampled expansion of human consciousness.

I shall accordingly treat books and paragraphs of books as scale models of America. For if in American history some ideal national self has had to contend from the outset with realities of time, biology, economics, and social custom, so in American literature the individual self has had to struggle into life through media of expression shaped by these realities. My demonstrations involve none of the usual connections between historical events and literary events, since I question the possibility of knowing what these are in relation to one another. Instead, I propose to measure this struggle for consciousness, personal and national, within the language of particular works. Sometimes, as in Cooper, the existence of the struggle is evident mostly in absurdities of style; at other times, as in Emerson, the struggle is merely evoked rather than made, as in Thoreau, the very substance of metaphor. Mark Twain tries to avoid the struggle, Huck Finn gets him into it, but he then drops Huck as a subject of interest in the very book named for him and turns his attention to a survey of the environmental forces within which not even a confused consciousness of freedom, like Huck's, can possibly come to full life. Later, Dreiser will derive his creative energy from a kind of fascinated surrender to the mysterious forces that in the City destroy freedom and even any consciousness of its loss.

The books which in my view constitute a distinctive American tradition within English literature are early, very often clumsy examples of a modernist impulse in fiction: they resist within their pages the forces of environment that otherwise dominate the world. Their styles have an eccentricity of defiance, even if the defiance shows sometimes as carelessness. Cooper, Emerson, Thoreau, Melville, Hawthorne, Mark Twain, James — they both resemble and serve their heroes by trying to create an environment of "freedom," though as writers their efforts must be wholly in language. American books are often written as if historical forces cannot possibly provide such an environment, as if history can give no life to "freedom," and as if only language can create the liberated place. The classic American writers try through style temporarily to free the hero (and the reader) from systems, to free them from the pressures of time, biology, economics, and from the social forces which are ultimately the undoing of American heroes and quite often of their creators. What distinguishes American heroes of this kind from those in the fiction of Mrs. Wharton, Dreiser, or Howells is that there is nothing within the real world, or in the systems which dominate it, that can possibly satisfy their aspirations. Their imagination of the self — and I speak now especially of heroes in Cooper, Melville, James — has no economic or social or sexual objectification; they tend to substitute themselves for the world. Initially and finally at odds with "system," perhaps their best definition is Henry James Sr.'s description of the artist as hero. In a passage, later given at some length, where he affirms a parallel between the writer, struggling to express himself in language, and the defiant hero, contending with the recalcitrant materials of reality, the artist is described as "the man of whatsoever function, who in fulfilling it obeys his own inspiration and taste, uncontrolled either by his physical necessities or his social obligations." The artist-hero may be, as he often is in American literature, an athlete, a detective, or a cowboy, his technical skills being as disciplined as the skills of art.

James's description might as easily come from Emerson, specifically from his essay "The Poet." It reflects a transcendentalist idea of style — not that style should mediate between the self and society but that it should emanate from the self as a leaf from a tree, expanding itself naturally to nourish, color, and become the world. Emerson himself, as "transparent eyeball," is only the first of the many similar figures in American literature who thus "swell" into shapes or defy the realities of space and time.

In works where this expansion of self occurs there is less a tendency to criticize existing environments — for that one would read Howells or Sinclair Lewis — than an effort to displace them. So that even at the moment of worldly defeat the hero has managed to create, like the exiled Coriolanus, at least the illusion of "a world elsewhere." Works like *Moby-Dick* or *The Ambassadors,* for example, are *designed* to make the reader feel that his ordinary world has been acknowledged, even exhaustively, only to be dispensed with as a source of moral or psychological standards. They are written so as finally not to be translatable into those standards, and their extravagances of language are an exultation in the exercise of consciousness momentarily set free. We can say of two American writers as different as Melville and James that both are quite willing, for themselves and for their heroes, to accept the appearance of failure in the interests of this free exercise of consciousness.

To make an environment in language that thwarts any attempts to translate that language into the terms of conventional environments is to write with a complexity that few even now are willing to allow to the novel or to any kind of prose. Indeed it is significant that most adverse criticism of, say, Melville or James, displays a marked failure to give requisite attention to the demanding styles by which these writers create an imaginary environment that excludes the standards of that "real" one to which most critics subscribe.

I am making a distinction between works that create through language an essentially imaginative environment for the hero and works that mirror an environment already accredited by history and society. This distinction is usually explained, more often than not explained away, by saying that the first kind of environment belongs to the romance and that the second belongs to the novel. Hawthorne provides, in his Preface to *The House of the Seven Gables*, the *locus classicus*:

> When a writer calls his work a Romance, it need hardly be observed that he wishes to claim a certain latitude, both as to its fashion and material, which he would not have felt himself entitled to assume had he professed to be writing a Novel. The latter form of composition is presumed to aim at a very minute fi-

delity, not merely to the possible, but to the probable and ordinary course of man's experience. The former — while, as a work of art, it must rigidly subject itself to laws, and while it sins unpardonably so far as it may swerve aside from the truth of the human heart — has fairly a right to present that truth under circumstances, to a great extent, of the writer's own choosing or creation. If he thinks fit, also, he may so manage his atmospherical medium as to bring out or mellow the lights and deepen and enrich the shadows of the picture. He will be wise, no doubt, to make a very moderate use of the privileges here stated, and, especially, to mingle the Marvellous rather as a slight, delicate, and evanescent flavor, than as any portion of the actual substance of the dish offered to the public. He can hardly be said, however, to commit a literary crime even if he disregard this caution.

Sorted out for us here are the two kinds of fictional environment I have been trying to describe: one might be called the provided environment, the other an invented environment. But it is regrettable that Hawthorne chose to elevate distinctions about environment, which is after all only one aspect of fiction, into distinctions between genres. Use of the terms "romance" and "novel" have in fact prevented rather than encouraged serious consideration of the American obsession with inventing environments that permit unhampered freedom of consciousness. Obsession is not too strong a word if English fiction is brought in for contrast. One of the first English novels comparable to the American fiction of civilization and the frontier is *Robinson Crusoe,* but it is indicative of the American emphases of Cooper, of Mark Twain, of Thoreau, though Thoreau gives a whole chapter of *Walden* to bourgeois considerations of economy, that Defoe's novel is a sort of idyllic parable of man's gaining merely economic control over an environment out of which he could try to make anything he chose. A true born Englishman, he has no interest whatever in the merely visionary possession of landscape, which a later chapter of this book traces throughout American literature. This comparison suggests what is, for other reasons, too, an inescapable conclusion: the strangeness of American fiction has less to do with the environment in which a novelist finds himself than with the environment he tries to create for his hero, usually his surrogate.

There is an evident reluctance on the part of American writers to admit that they intend to promote eccentricity both in the heroes of their works and in the environments provided for them. It is as if our writers wanted, in commenting on their own work and on the works of one another, to hide what they most wanted to do, and to hide their true intentions under disingenuous complaints that they are victims of historical necessity. They ask us to believe that the strange environments they create are a consequence not of their distaste for social, economic, and biological realities but of the fact that these aren't abundant enough in American life. Cooper, Hawthorne, James, and commentators who follow them, all suggest that they would be happier if the social "texture" of American life were "thicker" even while they make every sort of literary effort to escape

even the supposedly thin "texture" which American society does provide. In the passage from Hawthorne, in
similar passages from Cooper and James, the talk about
"romance" is always connected with the supposition
that America could not provide an environment which
sustained American novelists. "This country," Cooper
writes in his Preface to *Home as Found*, "in its ordinary
aspects, probably presents as barren a field to the writer
of fiction, and to the dramatist, as any other on earth; we
are not certain we might not say the most barren . . . .
It would be indeed a desperate undertaking, to think of
making anything interesting in the way of a *Roman de
Société* in this country." And it is from such arguments
that American writers and critics have made the by no
means necessary extrapolation that Americans of genius
were forced to write romances rather than novels.

The categorization of American fiction into novels,
and, more numerously, into romances, even when the
categories are made subtle by Richard Chase in *The
American Novel and Its Tradition* has tended to ob-
scure the more challenging questions: Are not certain
kinds of experience much harder to put into language
than other kinds? Are there not some states of consciousness that resist dramatic formulation, regardless of the
genre in which the effort is made, because in dialogue or
in actions they automatically become "like" some conventional states of consciousness that are less transcendental than perverse? When scenes occur in American
literature that by standards of ordinary life are foolish,
preposterous, or sexually irregular they are usually interpreted in one of three, all relatively unsatisfactory,
ways: they are translated into psycho-sexual terms with
the implication that because we have thereby discovered

something covert we have therefore revealed "more" than the obvious, idealistic, or ideological reading. Or they are discussed merely as metaphoric expressions of one or another recurrent myth in romantic or American literature, with little, usually no attention to the fact that the expression of this myth often does unwittingly raise questions about sex and psychology. Or they are much more simply disposed of with the observation that after all they belong to a romance, since of course they could not have occurred in a novel.

All three procedures, but noticeably the last, have the same basic deficiency: a tendency to treat experiences in fiction as if somehow they existed independently of the style which creates them and which creates, too, the environment in which these experiences make or do not make sense. It is as though we apprehended these experiences not through the media of language at this particular point or at that one, but within the baggy categories of "romance," or "myth," "realism," or "naturalism." The crucial problem for the best American writers is to evade all such categorizations and to find a language that will at once express and protect states of consciousness that cannot adequately be defined by conventional formulations even of more sophisticated derivation from Marx, Freud, or Norman O. Brown. The problem is stylistic. Quite locally so in the sounds and shapes of words. Genres have no instrumentality for expression, especially those of "novel" and "romance." These so-called genres have none of the ascertainable conventions of style that can legitimately be associated with such genres as the pastoral or the epic. One can see and hear language, see and hear the struggle in a voice to find a language appropriate to some mysterious state of consciousness; but no one has ever seen or heard language that necessarily belongs to a novel rather than a romance.

Once beyond the superficiality of genre criticism and the limitations of other more sophisticated categorizations, what is most interesting in American literature is the attempt in the writing to "build a world" wherein, say, even drunkenness might be the rule of the day. I mention drunkenness not only because it is a fairly common way of at least temporarily modifying one's relationship to customary environment. It is also William James's example when he is discussing in *Varieties of Religious Experience* a problem in life much the same as the problem I am considering in literature:

> Inner happiness and serviceability do not always agree. What immediately feels most 'good' is not always most 'true,' when measured by the verdict of the rest of experience. The difference between Philip drunk and Philip sober is the classic instance in corroboration. If merely 'feeling good' could decide, drunkenness would be the supremely valid human experience. But its revelations, however acutely satisfying at the moment, are inserted into an environment which refuses to bear them out for any length of time. The consequence of this discrepancy of the two criteria is the uncertainty which still prevails over so many of our spiritual judgments. There are moments of sentimental and mystical experience . . . that carry an enormous sense of inner authority and illumination with them when

they come. But they come seldom, and they do not come to every one; and the rest of life makes either no connection with them, or tends to contradict them more than it confirms them. Some persons follow more the voice of the moment in these cases, some prefer to be guided by the average results. Hence the sad discordancy of so many of the spiritual judgments of human beings. . . .

According to William James there is a necessary discontinuity between revelatory moments, always sporadic and infrequent, and the "environment" in which people ordinarily pass their time. In discovering the nature of environment, in life or in a book, we must, taking a hint from this passage, look not only at the way space is filled but also at the way time is customarily measured. The proportions of time authorized for any given activity, like getting drunk, are as important as "place" to our understanding of environment.

Though James is talking about careers in life, of Philip drunk and Philip sober, what he implies is still more decisively true of books. In literature environment is usually discussed in terms of place, or a social class, or a historical situation. This is a convenience too pleasant to give up. But it is only a convenience and it necessarily confuses what the books truly offer. As I use the word "environment," it means not the places named in a novel, like Chicago, let us say. Environment refers instead to the places filled in a book, filled with words that might indeed pretend to describe Chicago, but which in fact set a boundary on a wholly imaginary city in which the community of language shared by reader, characters, and author necessarily limits the possible shapes that action, persons, and language itself can assume. Nor does environment in a book mean, except in a most superficial sense, a time when events occur, be it 1966 or 1914. As I use the word "environment" with respect to a particular work, I mean the *proportions* of time that a writer feels he can give to some as against other kinds of events. In this sense, environment is really a derivative of such technical accomplishments as pacing and intensity, the weight of language at some points rather than at others. Why is it that often we remember vividly a particular scene that upon inspection turns out to have lasted only a few pages in a book of several hundred? From the answer to such a question we can discover that a writer could only give to moments of greatest illumination in his book, moments at which he seems to expend his genius most authentically, a small proportion of time and space as against what he felt required to give to "the rest of life."

Thinking of environment in American books as comparative units of space and time, a reader makes an obvious and very poignant discovery. What we remember about a book or a writer — and this is notably true in American literature — is often the smallest, momentary revelations that nonetheless carry, like the mystical experience to which William James alludes, an "enormous sense of inner authority." Much of this book is given over to a close look at such "passages" (the term "passages" could not be more apt) and to examining why they sometimes exist, with relation to the rest of the books in which they occur, much as do James's drunken or mystical experiences when these are "inserted into an environment which refuses to bear them out for any length of time." The rest of life, like the rest of a book, "tends to contradict them more than it confirms them."

The greatest American authors really do try, against the perpetually greater power of reality, to create an environment that might allow some longer existence to the hero's momentary expansions of consciousness. They try even when they are sure of failing, as Hawthorne was; they struggle for years in the face of failure, as Mark Twain did with his finest book, and as Melville did with most of his; and when they succeed, as James sometimes does, it is only that they may then be accused of neglecting the "realities" of sex, economics, or social history.

A novel as familiar as *Huckleberry Finn* is perhaps illustration enough of the problem of environment. Briefly, the book creates two environments for the hero, the raft and the shore. The environment of the shore is an investment in history and locale; Jim and Huck's few moments on the river, before they are joined by the King and the Duke, are a retreat from history; they are quite literally out of place and beyond economics. To remember the novel is spontaneously to remember the raft scenes, and yet looking back at the text we discover that the space and time given the scenes on the raft constitute less than a tenth of the whole, and that even on the raft Huck's mind is contaminated by the values of the shore. What Mark Twain discovered at the point of his famous and prolonged difficulties after Chapter xv was that even his limited effort to create an environment alternative to the shore had made his task impossible. He must, finally, "insert" Huck back into his customary environment. He must, in effect, destroy him. Huck as a character, created mostly in his soliloquies up through Chapter xv, is replaced by another figure, using the same name, but able to exist within the verbal world of the last two thirds of the novel, a world demonstrably less free than the verbal world or environment of the first third. *Huckleberry Finn* is a kind of history of American literature and it is altogether superior to most of what passes for histories of American literature. It is superior because it brings within its covers a conflict too often discussed as if it merely split American fiction, or the works of American writers, down the middle. On the one side we have the "romantic," and on the other we have the "realistic" or "naturalistic" schools. None of the interesting American novelists can be placed on either side of this dichotomy. Nearly all of them are written in protest against the environment of the "rest of life" which contradicts the dreams of their heroes and heroines. The distinction to be made is between those whose protests sometimes take the form of creating in their works an alternative environment, as James and sometimes Faulkner have tried to do, as Mark Twain for a while did do, and those for whom the environment of the real world simply overpowers, as it does in *Huckleberry Finn,* any effort of the imagination to transcend it. In this case the imagination, as in the novels of Dreiser and Edith Wharton, can only reproduce the effect of environment as force.

## II

The idea that through language it is possible to create environments radically different from those supported by economic, political, and social systems is one of the sustaining myths of any literature. It is a myth in one sense because it is historically invalid: the enormous contrivances of style called forth by this effort are themselves an admission that the environment thus created has an existence only in style. Not God, not religion, not reality, history, or nature, but style is its only authority. It is a myth in another sense because writers do want to believe, repetitively, despite history and their own experience, in the transcendent power of their own stylistic enterprise. The repetition and persistence of this myth has been especially evident in American literature for the obvious reason that for the only time in history men could, with the prospects of a new continent, actually believe in their power at last to create an environment congenial to an ideal self. American literature is thus full of images equivalent to the frontier. As Edwin Fussell shows, Walden is the West for Thoreau. On the pond he can build an environment for himself in which not only wilderness but also the civilizing technologies are made subservient to him. *Walden* is only one of the examples of something like an obsession in American literature with plans and efforts to build houses, to appropriate space to one's desires, perhaps to inaugurate therein a dynasty that shapes time to the dimensions of personal and familial history. Most of the houses in Cooper answer these ambitions, as does the Grangerford house in *Huckleberry Finn,* the House of the Seven Gables, Fawns in James's *Golden Bowl,* Sutpen's Hundred in Faulkner's *Absalom, Absalom!,* Silas Lapham's house, Gatsby's estate, and even the remade country house of Bellow's *Herzog.* Coincident with some of these are the American theorists of housing and of space, Horatio Greenough, Louis Sullivan, Frank Lloyd Wright, and that great historian of space, power, and architecture Henry Adams.

The building of a house is an extension and an expansion of the self, an act by which the self possesses environment otherwise possessed by nature. By an act of building, so the theorists I've mentioned would have it, it is possible to join forces with the powers of nature itself, to make its style your style. But this conjunction is possible only if the imagination and space are freed from the possessive power of all that is not nature: from systems of any kind that derive from society and history, from, often as not, "Europe."

From the outset American writers (or architects) who wanted in America to create environments in concert with the formative powers of nature found that they had first to rid themselves and America of styles imposed upon them by history. Even the men who dispossessed the Indian could only possess, could only *see* America through the styles and instrumentalities of the old world. According to Faulkner's Isaac McCaslin, the land was

> "already tainted even before any white man
> owned it by what Grandfather and his kind,
> his fathers, had brought into the new land
> which He had vouchsafed them out of pity and
> sufferance, on condition of pity and humility
> and sufferance and endurance, from that old
> world's corrupt and worthless twilight as
> though in the sailfuls of the old world's tainted
> wind which drove the ships — "

The theme of "possession" and of "dispossession," one of the subjects of Chapter II of this book, finds its greatest contemporary expression in *The Bear,* where the hero rejects both his historical and his economic inheritance so that he might live in an environment where time (his relation to family and family past) and space (the wilderness, and the plantation he is to inherit) are redeemed by his sacrifice of profit from either, his relinquishment both of a sexual and of an economic identity. In all respects he gives up the house of his ancestors.

The images of housing, of possession, and of achieving by relinquishment of one's inheritance some original relation to time and space — all these are parts of what we recognize in the characteristic career of American heroes and heroines. But all these images serve equally well to describe the activities of American writers and their relation to literary styles and conventions. Thus at the point in *Democratic Vistas* just before he claims that he "can conceive a community, today and here" where "perfect personalities without noise meet," Whitman complains, in a way almost tiredly conventional by 1871, that "Of course, in these States, for both man and woman, we must entirely recast the types of highest personality from what the oriental, feudal, ecclesiastical worlds bequeath us, and which yet possess the imaginative and aesthetic fields of the United States."

Whitman's critical utterances are an example of how aesthetic theories of literary independence and originality, the preoccupation of American writers from nearly the beginnings of our literature, are an analogue to the effort by American fictional heroes to free themselves from the conventions of historically rooted environ-

ments. Whitman in his poetry fashions a poetic style
wherein as both writer and hero of the poems he can be
the gregarious flirt and voyeur that he was. His is a style
in which the "I" escapes the limited relations permitted
in environments fostered by society and expands to include anything, which in his case means everything. In
quite other ways, the same omniverousness is evident in
the later James. There, the environment which is
James's style — an extraordinary invention in the history of language — makes it natural for the author to
have total entry into the consciousness of all of his characters. James's later novels have the quality of vast interior monologues with James playing all the parts at
will. Thoreau's *Walden* is perhaps more explicit than
any other American book about the connections between a defiant hero literally building a world of his
own — this is also, of course, the subject of *The Golden
Bowl* — and the writer who looks upon writing as anala-
gous to building. Like Whitman, and like the later
James, Thoreau *is* his style. His style is itself the hero of
the book: it is in substance the writer's self, the various
selves that he absorbs, and it is a mirror of the creative
originality of the hero-poet.

Significantly, in none of these books, not even when
they permit a dialogue, is there allowance made for a
style that is not the characteristic style of the author.
And I have purposely selected very familiar examples in
fiction, prose, and poetry. Necessarily, "perfect personalities without noise meet" in Whitman's charming picture: the only noise is the writer's own, speaking for
everyone. The artist becoming "God" through his creative activity is an ambition implicit in the whole idea of
creating environments where worldly distinctions

among persons are of no consequence. "Spring," in
*Walden* is a grotesque image of this process. It is an
account of Thoreau's vision of the "excrementitious"
flow of sand and vegetation in the season of rebirth
and a vision of himself within this flow as "but a
mass of thawing clay." Continually fluid, leading on to
shapes not yet apprehended and never to be fixed, "nature is "the laboratory of the Artist who made the
world and me." To nature as an artist Thoreau joins
his own plastic powers, his own activities as a poet-
maker. That is what he means by a "living" artist: "the
earth is not a mere fragment of dead history," he writes,
"stratum upon stratum like the leaves of a book,* to be
studied by geologists and antiquarians chiefly, but living
poetry like the leaves of a tree, which precede the flowers and fruit."

Here, as in Emerson's essay on "The Poet" and in his
admiration for the author of *Leaves of Grass,* is an early
form of an aesthetic which is sometimes thought to be
contemporary. It is an aesthetic so devoted to the *activity* of creation that it denies finality to the results of
that activity, its objects or formulations. Art is an action
not a product of action. To be creative is to discover
one's affinity with "God" and thereby one's superiority
to the works of men. Emerson's "Poet," like that version
of him who is Thoreau, therefore rejects even the solid-
ity of his own constructions, of his own created environments. No wonder American writers have always been

---

* This expression, or naming, Emerson writes, "is not art but a second
nature grown out of the first as a leaf out of a tree," a figure that in
our own century has found its way not only into the architectural
theories of Louis Sullivan but also into his drawings of compound leaf
forms to illustrate the organic and functional principles of *A System
of Architectural Ornament.*

outspoken in praise of self-contradiction, of "whim," and repetition. Self-contradiction suggests the unfinished life within the always expanding frontiers of the self — "do I contradict myself?/very well then I contradict myself,/(I am large, I contain multitudes)" — while repetition allows for endless variations within single things. There are at least thirteen of Wallace Stevens's blackbirds as well as thirteen ways of looking at one of them, and the third of Miss Stein's roses is, by the very act of naming it, not the second and not the first. Even any so-called "American" style would be a prison, if we accept the dictate of Emerson that "every thought is also a prison; every heaven is also a prison."

Something that in historically credited environments has a place and function is not even recognizable in that other environment of the artist which exists in a continually fluid state, continually transforming itself into new and mysterious forms. The notion has informed the most popular idioms about America. The metaphor of America as a melting-pot, for example, implies that the final product will, like Emerson's Poet, be a composite figure who "stands among partial men for the complete man." Emerson's Poet can have no established nationality; he is not imagined as having even a particular occupation, including the occupation of poet as we normally think of it. He is supposed to be simply and magnificently himself in whatever he chooses to do. The role of the artist is clarified a good deal by Emerson's friend and contemporary Henry James, Sr. in an almost unknown short lecture, already mentioned, in *Moralism and Christianity*:

> Who, then, is the perfect or divine man, the
> man who actually reconciles in himself all the

conflicting elements of humanity? Is any such man actually extant? If so, where shall we find him?

We find him in the aesthetic man, or Artist. But now observe that when I speak of the aesthetic man or Artist, I do not mean the man of any specific function, as the poet, painter, or musician. I mean the man of whatsoever function, who in fulfilling it obeys his own inspiration or taste, uncontrolled either by his physical necessities or his social obligations. He alone is the Artist, whatever be his manifest vocation, whose action obeys his own internal taste or attraction, uncontrolled either by necessity or duty. The action may perfectly consist both with necessity and duty; that is to say, it may practically promote both his physical and social welfare; but these must not be its animating principles, or he sinks at once from the Artist into the artisan. The artisan seeks to gain a livelihood or secure an honorable name. He works for bread, or for fame, or for both together. The Artist abhors these ends, and works only to show forth that immortal beauty whose presence constitutes his inmost soul. He is vowed to Beauty as the bride is vowed to the husband, and Beauty reveals herself to him only as he obeys his spontaneous taste or attraction.

The reason accordingly why the painter, the poet, the musician, and so forth, have so long monopolized the name of Artist, is, not because Art is identical with these forms of action, for it is identical with no specific forms,

but simply because the poet, painter, and so
forth, more than any other men, have thrown
off the tyranny of nature and custom, and followed the inspirations of genius, the inspirations of beauty, in their own souls. These men
to some extent have sunk the service of nature
and society in the obedience of their own private attractions. They have merged the search
of the good and the true in that of the beautiful, and have consequently announced a divinity as yet unannounced either in nature or society. To the extent of their consecration, they
are priests after the order of Melchisedec, that
is to say, a priesthood which, not being made
after the law of a carnal commandment, shall
never pass away. And they are kings, who reign
by a *direct* unction from the Highest. But the
priest is not the altar, but the servant of the
altar; and the king is not the Highest, but a
servant of the Highest. So painting, poetry, is
not Art, but the servant and representative of
Art. Art is divine, universal, infinite. It therefore exacts to itself infinite forms or manifestations, here in the painter, there in the actor;
here in the musician, there in the machinist;
here in the architect, there in the dancer; here
in the poet, there in the costumer. We do not
therefore call the painter or poet, Artist, because painting or poetry is a whit more essential to Art than ditching is, but simply because
the painter and poet have more frequently exhibited the life of Art by means of a hearty in-
subjection to nature and convention.

When, therefore, I call the Divine Man, or God's image in creation, by the name of Artist, the reader will not suppose me to mean the poet, painter, or any other special form of man. On the contrary, he will suppose me to mean that infinite and spiritual man whom all these finite functionaries represent indeed, but whom none of them constitutes, namely, the man who in every visible form of action acts always from his inmost self, or from attraction, and not from necessity or duty. I mean the man who is a law unto himself, and ignores all outward allegiance, whether to nature or society. This man may indeed have no technical vocation whatever, such as poet, painter, and the like, and yet he will be none the less sure to announce himself. The humblest theatre of action furnishes him a platform. I pay my waiter so much a day for putting my dinner on the table. But he performs his function in a way so entirely *sui generis,* with so exquisite an attention to beauty in all the details of the service, with so symmetrical an arrangement of the dishes, and so even an adjustment of everything to its own place, and to the hand that needs it, as to shed an almost epic dignity upon the repast, and convert one's habitual "grace before meat" into a spontaneous tribute, instinct with a divine recognition.

The charm in this case is not that the dinner is all before me, where the man is bound by his wages to place it. This every waiter I have had has done just as punctually as this man, which

attests that in doing it, he is not thinking either of earning his wages, or doing his duty toward me, but only of satisfying his own conception of beauty with the resources before
him. The consequence is that the pecuniary
relation between us emerges in a higher one.
He is no longer the menial, but my equal or
superior, so that I have felt, when entertaining
doctors of divinity and law, and discoursing
about divine mysteries, that a living epistle
was circulating behind our backs, and quietly
ministering to our wants, far more apocalyptic
to an enlightened eye than any yet contained
in books.

The ease with which the elder James finds the artist in
occupations as mundane as waiting on table is one indication that an essentially Emersonian concept of style
involves much more than a standard merely of literary
performance. Emerson himself remarks that "poets are
thus liberating gods." Believing with James that poets
"more than any other men, have thrown off the tyranny of nature," Emerson also used the title Poet to
designate anyone of any occupation who in the exercise
of it fully realizes the self or the selves that are in him.
Emerson and Henry James Sr. affirm what could in any
case be inferred from the great American books: an
identification of the writer, idealized as a liberator of
consciousness, with the heroes of a more practical,
worldly, and physical achievement. These heroes may be
men of "whatsoever function," but in a significant number of cases they too are "liberators." Deerslayer shows
his daring mostly in freeing his friends and himself from

captivity, so does Huck Finn, and so, too does Faulkner's Charles Mallison of *Intruder in the Dust*. The stories of Poe and of Melville are full of imprisonments and efforts at liberation, while James, like Hawthorne, evolved a style meant to liberate his heroes from those, like the governess in *The Turn of the Screw,* who would "fix," imprison, or "know" others.

The situation can be described in terms of rather crude historical progression. It could be said that the theories of literary and stylistic independence, articulated if not originated by Emerson, were gradually transmuted into an ideal of heroic character asserting its independence of oppressive environments and of prefabricated social styles. So, too, the difficulties of Cooper and Emerson in achieving stylistic independence are translated, as it were, by Hawthorne, and increasingly by American novelists after him, into the central dramatic situation of their works. In this, as in many other ways, Salinger's Holden Caulfield is a merely stock character enacting the American hero's effort, more significantly illustrated by Isabel Archer, to express the natural self rather than merely to represent, in speech and manner, some preordained social type.

Defiance of convention by a writer in his style or by a character in his actions is necessarily part of the effort to create a new environment or to escape the confinements of an old one. Again, we can think of the sequence of American literature almost novelistically, each chapter modifying the concerns tentatively revealed in a previous one. Thus, when Cooper in 1828 remarks in *Notions of a Travelling Bachelor* that "it is quite obvious that, so far as taste and forms alone are concerned, the literature of England and that of America must be fash-

ioned after the same models," he is rather passively describing a cultural situation that was later to be the
provocation for Emerson's "The American Scholar" and
for Whitman's *Democratic Vistas,* where, forty-three
years after Cooper, Whitman would still be complaining
that "as yet America has artistically originated nothing."
Cultural dependence in Mark Twain became the object
of satire, though he was himself its victim, and it was
fable-ized in Henry James's international novels, both
early, in *The Europeans,* and late, in *The Ambassadors.*
In summary, Cooper describes conditions which in Emerson fostered a myth of newness, a myth that gets enacted humanly by Huck Finn, a character whose consciousness exceeds the "styles" to which the book as well
as Huck are ultimately forced to surrender.

Recognizing the chasm between a fully developed
consciousness of self and the socially accepted styles by
which that self can get expressed, Henry James developed a style which pays almost no deference to what we
recognize as the language of ordinary social intercourse.
It is a style that instead gives credence and support to
extraordinary, almost grotesque expansions of consciousness, grotesque in the sense that the consciousness
thus rendered is very often a mixture of James's own in-
trusive sensibility and the generally more limited ones
of the characters of his later books. But even James was
not able wholly to protect such heroes from questions
prompted by the reader's commitment to a society and a
language existent outside of James's books. There have,
as a result, been endless debates about the significance
in psychological and social terms of the renunciations of
any customary forms of happiness at the end of nearly
all his novels, noticeably at the end of *The Portrait of a
Lady, The Spoils of Poynton, The Wings of the Dove,*

and *The Ambassadors.* The problem is evidence of the distinctive American quality of James. The crisis in the most interesting American works often occurs at those moments when the author tries to externalize the inner consciousness of his hero, tries to insert it, to borrow William James's metaphor, into social and verbal environments that won't sustain it. And the crisis is confronted not only by the heroes but also by their creators when it comes to conceiving of some possible resolution to the conflict of inner consciousness or some suitable external reward for it.

Describing the situation in images which most often embody it in American literature, we can say that American writers are at some point always forced to return their characters to prison. They return them to "reality" from environments where they have been allowed most "nakedly" to exist, environments created by various kinds of stylistic ingenuity. They "clothe" them and subject them to questions of a social and sexual nature which it has been their and their creator's intention to avoid. When Isaac, in Faulkner's *The Bear,* enters the woods as a boy of ten, for example, it is, we are told, as if he is going back in time, leaving any historically formed environment. He feels that he is witnessing his own birth, "the wagon progressing not by its own volition but by attrition of their intact yet fluid circumambience, drowsing, earless, almost lightless." This image is contrived to imitate the movement of a baby out of the womb and into the world, the hero's imagined denudation being a prelude not only to his eloquent later choice of what he calls "dispossession," but to the necessities which accompany that choice: of a lonely, sexless, childless life.

In a companion story to *The Bear, Delta Autumn,*

Faulkner gives a savage rightness to the question asked
of Isaac, now an old man, by the mulatto mistress of his
nephew: what, she asks, can he know about love.
The issue Faulkner recognizes here, and has the genius
to exploit, is nearly everywhere a tension in American
literature: the tension of bringing into conjunction the
environment of nakedness, where there is no encum-
brance to the expression of the true inner self, and the
environment of costume, of outer space occupied by society and its fabrications. The utter simplicity of Gatsby's room is another example of what one might call the
environment of inner space, intended to show the mean-
inglessness of the festooned life that Gatsby presents to
the world. The configuration in Fitzgerald has already
been anticipated, of course, in the nakedness enjoyed by
Huck and Jim, when Huck does not have to go out in
the disguises by which he "fits into" society. Similarly, a
return to "nakedness" is also for Emerson the virtue of
the woods: where "a man casts off his years as a snake his
slough, and at what period soever of life is always a
child," even while his own style has often a contrasting,
sometimes debilitating "dress" and elegance.* And

* The romantic tradition by which the virtues of nakedness get connected with the virtues of childhood is understandably translated into
distinctly American educational theories designed to preserve the style
of youth and childhood. Among the relevant texts would be Louis
Sullivan's *Kindergarten Chats*, John Dewey, *In the School and Society*,
and A. F. Chamberlain who in *The Child: A Study in the Evolution of
Man* makes an explicit connection between childhood, as one of the
best "furnishings" of man, and the creation of art. "Youth was fur-
nished in the order of natural development to the animal as a means
of utilizing and controlling the wealth of innate instincts and impulses
in a new and higher fashion . . . man especially possess(es) youth because it was necessary to create art (and civilization) from instincts
through the transforming power of play." See Sherman Paul, *Louis
Sullivan: An Architect in American Thought*, Prentice-Hall, 1962,
Chapter IV.

while Thoreau is not generally credited with having had an influence on Henry James, it seems likely that in *The Portrait of a Lady,* Thoreau's disquisition on "Clothing" was on the periphery of James's satiric intention when, to Madame Merle's belief that "we are each of us made up of a cluster of appurtenances," he lets Isabel respond that

> "I don't know whether I succeed in expressing myself, but I know that nothing else expresses me. Nothing that belongs to me is any measure of me; on the contrary it's a limit, a barrier, and a perfectly arbitrary one. Certainly the clothes which, as you say, I choose to wear, don't express me; and heaven forbid they should!"

> "You dress very well," interposed Madame Merle, skilfully.

> "Possibly; but I don't care to be judged by that. My clothes may express the dressmaker, but they don't express me. To begin with, it's not my own choice that I wear them; they are imposed upon me by society."

Madame Merle's answer — "Should you prefer to go without them?" — terminates the discussion. But meanwhile James shows his willingness consciously to expose his heroine to standards which usually embarrass those earlier American writers who share many of Isabel's ideas and indulge themselves in many of the images she also uses. Of course the Emersonianism here is Isabel's not James's, whose allegiances were, in any case, as much to the social as to the transcendental expressions of the self. But the passage nonetheless illustrates James's tenderness for ideals of *self*-expression as against expression

by which the self is filtered through representative or
acquired styles. This concern passes to him from Emerson (and James's father) through the whole body of
American literature.

To a degree that forces on us a critically retrospective
look at American literature, James recognizes the impossibility of "naked" self-expression, the illusion that,
like Emerson's "Poet," one can "turn the world to
glass." In one sense his novels are about the disaster of
assuming that within the environments provided by society there can be any allowance of space for the free
expansion of the inner self. Opposed to any such transla-
tions and metamorphoses of the self are realities represented not only by the fashion of wearing clothing.
Standing in opposition also, are the fashions of language, the elemental social necessities of life implicit
even in the agreement to use language in its inherited
and publicly accepted forms.

There are two characteristics of language and of literature that are at odds with the Emersonian ideal of
building a world of one's own. First of all, there is the
acceptance by any writer, and conspicuously by Emerson himself, of certain decorums in his address to an imagined audience, of certain shared suppositions — "this
is how an essay sounds" or "this is an acceptable voice
for a novel." The "I" that is heard in the voice is therefore unlikely to be the same "I" that is projected by images of the liberated self or the Artist. Second, there is
the convention in nineteenth-century fiction of dialogue, even if the dialogue is sometimes wholly recol-
lected or imagined in a single mind. Subscription to the
convention of dialogue means that in American fiction
certain ideas that sound absurd in anything but mono-

logue or soliloquy become the subject of conversation. Such dialogue, notably in Cooper, Hawthorne, and Melville, is quite often pointlessly stilted and literary. It is as if these writers felt that dialogue was forced upon them. In some measure it was, since dialogue presupposes an accommodation to aspects of reality for which these writers have an evident distaste: the necessity of social intercourse, the acceptance of literary and social conventions in the definition of the Self, the acceptance of other selves *as* other. Cooper and Melville, for instance, want to believe in the possibility that the self can expand not merely in the presence of natural force but also in the company of other people, that the same self can carry on polite conversations and be, in one form or other, something as non-human as a "transparent eyeball."

Stressing these essential facts about American literature, one has to confront some of the issues raised by Leslie Fiedler. I want to say at the outset that *Love and Death in the American Novel* is to my mind probably the best single book on American fiction ever written, and it is surely unsurpassed in its definition of Gothicism as a characteristic of that fiction. The book has been most resented for its purported emphasis on sexual perversity in American literature and in its use of this as an index to certain historical and cultural tensions. Actually Fiedler is altogether less daring and less insistent on this aspect of our literature than was Lawrence in his much earlier study, and he is in no sense as moralistic about sex as a literary component. If Huckleberry Finn were the boy next door, it would probably hurt him more to call him homo-erotic than to call him Faustian, but Fiedler knows that as applied to fictional characters either designation is mythic, not accusatory. What he forgets is that either designation is also destructive of what Huck more *particularly* offers us in his style or in his contribution to a novel so full of the struggle for verbal consciousness. One of the troubles with Fiedler's argument is that it is often initiated by an emphasis on "character," as if "character" existed in nineteenth-century American fiction in the unfractured form it usually takes in English fiction of the same period. He can therefore insist on the significance of certain acts or words as if they refer to "character" and its psychological structure when more often these acts and words belong instead to some larger metaphorical significance in a work to which sexual psychology is merely incidental or irrelevant. Huck and Jim lying naked together on the raft are in fact looking less at each other than at the stars or the river; their nakedness expresses less about their feelings for each other than about their assertion of freedom, as necessary for the white boy as for the Negro slave, from the world of costume, of Style.

Fiedler's work is a brilliant example of mythopoeic criticism given its fullest exposition three years before *Love and Death in the American Novel* by Northrop Frye in *Anatomy of Criticism.* In Fiedler as in Frye is the assumption that mythopoeic and archetypal constructs have some existence more historically and scientifically demonstrable than the existence of a so-called text. The "text" thus becomes, as Fiedler is happy to assert, "merely one of the contexts of a piece of literature," though this creates a problem in semantics which it is not my responsibility here to unravel.* Fiedler's

---

* See my review of *Love and Death in the American Novel* in *Daedalus,* Winter 1961, pp. 167–72.

methods are not essentially different from those of other commentators who are concerned with recurrences of literary motifs and with the elaboration of these into archetypes or myths. It may be more provocative but it is not more or less valid to reduce American literature to certain versions of sexual dislocation than to reduce it to versions of Eden, Christ, or the Frontier. Because even granting the rewards of mythopoeic readings, one then wants to go on to something more important: an investigation of the career of *topoi* in their passage through inhospitable verbal contexts, through conventions of expression and through literary structures that distort them, giving even to a commonplace romantic image of "nakedness" some peripheral suggestions of "innocent homosexuality." The suggestions *are* peripheral, however—a consequence of literary rather than psychological conditions. What is centrally important is the evidence almost everywhere in American literature of an idealistic effort to free the heroes' and the readers' consciousness from categories not only of conventional moralities but also of mythopoeic interpretation.

The result is a struggle to create through language an environment in which the inner consciousness of the hero-poet can freely express itself, an environment in which he can sound publicly what he privately is. Emphasis on the element of struggle in giving even a temporary existence to this environment means that the archetypes, images, themes, or ideas that have been the main concern of most recent studies of American literature are in this study only of incidental or procedural use. In treating such items as the "eye," "nakedness," "infancy," "newness," my concern is with the shapes given such images and ideas when they are under the pressure of various stylistic contexts. What immediately strikes a reader of almost any American classic, of which *Moby-Dick* might be an example, is that his attention is grasped less by images or the significances attached to them, both being usually obvious and often banal, than by the peculiar archness with which they get expressed. *Moby-Dick* is not written as cryptography but as mystery. The agitations of voice, the playfulness through which symbols emerge and then dissolve, the mixtures of incantatory, Biblical, polite, and vernacular language in this and other American books — these are what demand our attention altogether more than do ideas or themes extracted by critics in the interest of tidying up what is mysterious or confused. Marius Bewley's title for a book on American literature, *The Eccentric Design*, therefore promises that he will come much nearer the central problems of that literature than does the title of a more recent book by Tony Tanner, *The Reign of Wonder*, with its implied emphasis on intentions, on ways of perceiving in American literature rather than on ways of expressing what is perceived. However, Mr. Tanner's book turns out to be full of very rewarding speculations; it traces important continuities among American books with tact and unusual discrimination. What is more, he is alert to the problem of stylization, notably in vernacular literature and in the prose-poetry of Gertrude Stein and Henry James. But while showing us how "nearly all American writers have found it difficult to move beyond the first step [of seeing like children] to find satisfactory forms," he then admits that "This phenomenon poses a problem which is obviously beyond the scope of this book."

Trying myself to meet this problem, to make it, in fact, the subject of this book, I share Mr. Tanner's nervousness. The critic who offers the most help is D. H. Lawrence in *Studies in Classic American Literature,* probably the crucial study of American literature. Such a claim can be justified even though the book manages to ignore Emerson, Mark Twain, and Henry James. It illustrates how a work of critical genius can cover a subject even while neglecting large areas of it. The explanation, in this instance, is that Lawrence was himself by temperament an "American" writer working within the conventions of English literature. He was not only responsive to the main lines of force in American literature; he himself accelerated them. In Lawrence, with a degree of consciousness never attained by any American writer, are the struggles, difficulties, and tensions that went into the writing of the best American books. So much did he feel these tensions that perhaps his clearest expression of them comes when he is talking not about American writing at all, but about his own. Thus in describing what he is trying to do in *Women in Love,* he speaks of that novel as an effort to find a mode of expression for ideas that are struggling into a life which language, and only language, can give them:

> Man struggles with his unborn needs and fulfilment. New unfoldings struggle up in torment in him, as buds struggle forth from the midst of a plant. Any man of real individuality tries to know and to understand what is happening, even in himself, as he goes along. This struggle for verbal consciousness should not be

left out in art. It is a very great part of life. It is
not superimposition of a theory. It is the passionate struggle into conscious being.

We are now in a period of crisis. Every man
who is acutely alive is acutely wrestling with
his own soul. The people that can bring forth
the new passion, the new idea, this people will
endure. Those others, that fix themselves in
the old idea, will perish with the new life
strangled unborn within them. Men must
speak out to one another.

In point of style, fault is often found with
the continual, slightly modified repetition.
The only answer is that it is natural to the author; and that every natural crisis in emotion
or passion or understanding comes from this
pulsing, frictional to-and-fro which works up
to culmination.

The notion that to bring forth a new passion or a new
idea involves verbal struggle against established forms is
given a somewhat ironic confirmation by the fact that
the notion is itself one of the most persistent conventions of literature. Stylistic revolution is not the exclusive product of any particular historical situation, or the
exclusive property of any national literature. If it seems
to belong to American writing at the time of Cooper
and Emerson, it also belongs to the America of Hamlin
Garland and later of Hemingway. If it belonged to English and American poetry when Pound wrote "Make It
New," to English poetry when Wordsworth and Coleridge wrote the Preface to the second edition of the
*Lyrical Ballads,* it also belonged to Samuel Daniel, some

two hundred years earlier, when he announced the fitness of English for rhymed verse. When Gertrude Stein laid down the law that "A rose is a rose is a rose" she was being repetitious with an intention already described. She probably did not intend also to be almost directly repetitious of Emerson in "Self Reliance":

> Man is timid and apologetic; he is no longer upright; he dares not say "I think," "I am," but quotes some saint or sage. He is ashamed before the blade of grass or the blowing rose. These roses under my window make no reference to former roses or to better ones; they are for what they are; they exist with God to-day. There is no time to them. There is simply the rose. . . .

In declaring the freedom of words from the significances which history has imposed on them even a writer as notoriously original as Miss Stein finds herself an imitator.

One struggle in American literature is to assert against conventional styles another kind of style that has been defined, out of Emerson and Whitman, by Louis Sullivan when he referred to style as "a consistent and definite expansion of pronounced personality." This struggle cannot wholly be explained simply by reference to some particular historical phenomenon, even one as staggering as the offering to men's imagination of a new world. All we can say is that American literature does offer the most persistent, the most poignantly heroic example of a recurrent literary compulsion, not at all confined to our literature, to believe in the possibilities of a new style. The new American style was meant to release

hitherto unexpressed dimensions of the self into space
where it would encounter none of the antagonistic social systems which stifle it in the more enclosed and cultivated spaces of England and of English books, the
spaces from which Lawrence escaped to the American
West.

Paradoxically, I know of no deeper penetration of this
central core of American literature than D. H. Lawrence's *St. Mawr*. It might seem merely ingenious to expand a critical proposition about American writing,
most of it of the nineteenth century, by analysis of a novella, an English novella at that, published in 1925. But
in fact, criticism, including Lawrence's *Studies,* has no
where confronted the problem I have been describing
with anything like the comprehensive genius exhibited
in *St. Mawr.* The story not only gives life to these problems; it also shows us, with a subtlety possible only,
perhaps, in a fictional dramatization, their enormous *literary* consequences. Once again the struggles going on
in American writing of the last century become the
fictional subject of later, so-called modern literature:
Lawrence demonstrates the difficulty, in environments
conventionalized by social and literary formulations, of
trying to find a voice, a personal style appropriate to
what he calls in the story the "onward pushing spirit."
Especially during that half of the story set in England,
this personal voice tries to be heard within the environments not simply of social forms but also within a language and conversational mode derivative of them. Except for what can be borrowed from literature and myth,
this social language is all his characters have as an instrument for defining that "spirit" and for entering into
dialogue with it.

*St. Mawr* is a kind of gathering of the motifs we have
so far been considering in classic American literature
and which are to some extent defined in Lawrence's
*Studies,* published over a year before, in 1923, but written within the period dating from 1917. Lawrence's
immersion in American literature is everywhere evident
in the story. The heroine, Lou Witt, living in England
with her mother and married to an Australian named
Rico, chooses, like many American heroes and heroines
before her, to disassociate herself from a polite society
and from a marriage, both parodied in the opening
pages, and to find renewal in the wilderness. She retreats
to the New Mexican desert, there to find a spirit "that
wants her." The geographical movement of the story has
obvious historical and literary precedents: from old to
new worlds, from England (the "close, hedged-and-
fenced English landscape. Everything enclosed, enclosed
to stifling") to Mexico (where "The great circling landscape lived its own life"), from a land without the opportunities proffered by unfilled space ("Not a space,
not a speck of this country that wasn't humanized, occupied by the human claim") to a landscape for which
"man did not exist." But before this geographical evocation of two worlds, Lou has already contrived them in
her imagination and has done so in a manner which,
again, suggests a classic feature of American literature:
when she first sees St. Mawr, an equestrian Moby-Dick, a
domesticated Big Ben, the horse "seemed to look at her
out of another world." While imagining this "other"
world, she can, like Thoreau, or Faulkner's heroes, or
Hemingway in his sporting or hunting stories, or Melville's Ahab, think of those around her in hierarchies
that appeal not to social institutions but rather to the

mysterious powers potent but thwarted in animal life. Lewis, the groom, thereby becomes elevated above her husband Rico, by "the aristocracy of invisible powers, the greater influences, nothing to do with human society."

Lou's effort to promote the secret powers of St. Mawr within the context of English mannered society can only find a voice in the first half of the story that is largely destructive and satiric. The burden of this satiric effort is at first carried mostly by her mother, Mrs. Witt. Her ironies are full of a self-loathing which Lou recognizes as a doomed alternative to the deadening social chic of her husband. But once St. Mawr has revealed himself in Texas as no more than a fawning stud, Lou finds in the landscape of New Mexico, in something no human being has tamed, a further call not merely to criticism of human society but to potencies beyond it. She tries to imagine for herself some creative alternative both to society and to the ironic-satiric treatment of it in which she had joined Mrs. Witt while both were entrapped within the terms and vocabularies of a social set. In a sense *St. Mawr* includes within itself the two attitudes toward existent environments which I've located in American literature: the one imitative, often satiric, often critical, but essentially submissive, in being merely corrective, to the necessary reality of established society; the other creative, daring, often ridiculous in the effort to express a creative ideal of alternative environment where the self can unite its powers with presumably harmonious natural forces.

Where Lawrence is most English in the story is in the degree to which even at the end he finds it necessary to be skeptical of the possibilities Lou is affirming. The skepticism expresses itself most noticeably in his never consorting fully with her tendencies as a symbolist: he himself never confirms the importance she assigns to St. Mawr or to the New Mexican landscape. Whatever support her symbolisms receive from his writing or from his narrative voice is in the marvelous beauty of his descriptions. If she is a symbolist, he more accurately displays what Gertrude Stein meant by remarking that "Description is explanation": the power and magnificence of landscape and of animal life is precisely, so Lawrence implies, that it is *not* available as metaphor. Lawrence's place in the book is a clarified version of Melville's in *Moby-Dick* when it comes to his subscribing to the symbolist tendencies of the central character. Skepticism of this kind, however, need not and does not modify the grandeurs of description in which Melville and Lawrence like to indulge. The admiration of the writers in both cases goes not to the possible accuracy of a symbolist perspective but only to the heroic nobility of incentive behind it, its creative responsiveness to the things of this world.

In the tradition of American romantic literature, Lawrence values the redemptive power of imagination even when its particular exertions are preposterous. The effort, the struggle to change the world, to alter even the laws of nature here, as in Emerson and in all of James, brings rewards only to the imagination and to the consciousness of participants and witnesses, rewards without any practical benefit or visible objectification. The struggle may be with the alien forces in nature that Emerson did not feel it necessary to acknowledge so fully as did Melville, but it is also with those inheritances of old thinking, of old formulas, and of language itself which Emerson continually laments, with no illusions that it is ever possible fully to escape from them.

While most of what I would call the American aspects of *St. Mawr* are altogether implicit, Lawrence seems anxious almost to signal the similarities (and differences) between himself and Emerson in the interpolated story of the New England woman. The story testifies to the historical frequency as well as to the Americanness of the situation in which Lou finds herself at the end of *St. Mawr*. The woman's story suggests, for one thing, that the struggle of the heroic self for a congenial environment involves no simple geographical movement from the civilization of Europe to the wilderness of America. The old world has so efficiently claimed for itself the civilized areas of the new that the woman must move still further into the continent in search of harmony with natural rather than with social forces. With her husband, a man as unbelieving a witness to the spiritual benefits of the enterprise as is Mrs. Witt, the New England woman moved to the ranch, bringing to that wilderness a "New England belief in a world ultimately all for love," and an assurance that she can find confirmation of this belief in "nature." Trying like Deerslayer paradoxically to bring civilization to a wilderness which is also her retreat from civilization (she tries to introduce water taps and to exterminate the rats), she is quite explicitly defined by Lawrence as someone trying to create or to "build" a world in the face of savagery. Though she fails ("she could not even keep her speech") she represents for Lawrence the positive virtue of effort, of struggle for its own sake, against the killing extremes of system, on the one side, and, on the other, the lowest stages of savage creation. "And all the time," Lawrence writes in a voice which has none of the ironic tinge it usually carries in this story, "man has to rouse himself afresh, to cleanse the new accumulations of refuse. To win from the crude wild nature the victory and the power to make another start, and to cleanse behind him the century-deep deposits of layer upon layer of refuse: even of tin cans." As in American literature, even the best efforts of the characters in Lawrence's fiction bring no practical benefits. Success is inward and invisible, an expansion of consciousness *in* the self. That this expansion on the part of the hero might ultimately have some renovating effect upon society is a hope more pronounced in Lawrence than in any American book that comes to mind, including Faulkner's *The Bear*. But some such renovation is implicit, in the very degree to which American writers strive in their styles, as Lawrence does, to be "poets," "liberating gods" of the confined consciousness of the reader.

*St. Mawr* is an astonishing feat in varieties and modulations of style precisely because Lawrence is so anxious to show how nearly impossible it is to be freed of those organizations of language, literary and social, within which human consciousness has chosen to define itself. He gives far greater proportionate attention to his characters' existence in language than to their sexual existence. At the end of *St. Mawr* it is made perhaps needlessly clear by the very name of the ranch — Las Chivas, or she-goats — and by the insistence on the pre-sexual horror of the savage landscape that Lou and her mother are paying a heavy human and psychological price, as do all similar American heroes, for their rejections and choices of environment.

Lawrence's irreducible Englishness is most apparent,

however, in making Lou's situation significantly unlike
that of any comparable American hero: at the end, communing with the landscape from which "stillness
speaks," she is still not alone and must herself enter into
human converse. Mrs. Witt is with her, is given indeed
the final lines of the story. Thus at the very end Lou is
forced into dialogue, into some definition of her inward
state that makes some sense to the older, socially adept,
practically minded woman. "Freedom" in Lawrence, for
Lou as for Birkin, who tries to make sense of himself to Ursula at the end of *Women in Love,* "freedom" means, as he puts it, "freedom together." In this
modification on the theme of retreat and solitude, Lawrence exposes his American tendencies to certain elemental biological and social realities that English fiction never completely eludes even in this century.
There is in Lawrence no evasion of these realities either
by allowing the hero to define himself in soliloquy,
rather than in dialogue, or by a self-annihilating claim
to Oneness or Allness. Whatever his characters express,
even in talk to themselves, carries in its sounds some
telltale mark of social place and history, some element
of the established environment against which they and
the book are still struggling at the end. Some of Lawrence's most grotesquely conventionalized types are allowed to pay verbal court to the Laurentian virtues,
but their sounds, overstuffed with chic or "thinking"
or academicism, betray them, as when Hermione de-
livers her classroom lecture in *Women in Love,* when
Cartwright phrases his admiration for the god Pan, or
when Laura talks to Lou about St. Mawr and about the
"very few people one can talk *really* simply with."

The extraordinary degrees of modulation in the story,
requiring altogether as much attention as would any

comparable work of poetry like *The Waste Land*, is
meant even at the very end to show that Lou cannot
wholly escape the environment she has left behind her
in Europe. Her final speech has in it the tainted sounds
of the fashionableness and literariness we have heard in
Laura and Cartwright:

> "Very well, daughter. You will probably
> spend your life keeping to yourself."
> "Do you think I mind! There's something
> else for me, mother. There's something else
> even that loves me and wants me. I can't tell
> you what it is. It's a spirit. And it's here, on this
> ranch. It's here, in this landscape. It's some-
> thing more real to me than men are, and it
> soothes me, and it holds me up. I don't know
> what it is, definitely. It's something wild, that
> will hurt me sometimes and will wear me
> down sometimes. I know it. But it's something
> big, bigger than men, bigger than people, big-
> ger than religion. It's something to do with
> wild America. And it's something to do with
> me. It's a mission, if you like. I am imbecile
> enough for that! — But it's my mission to keep
> myself for the spirit that is wild, and has
> waited so long here: even waited for such as
> me. Now I've come! Now I'm here. Now I am
> where I want to be: with the spirit that wants
> me. — And that's how it is. And neither Rico
> nor Phoenix nor anybody else really matters to
> me. They are in the world's back yard. And I
> am here, right deep in America, where there's
> a wild spirit wants me, a wild spirit more than
> men. And it doesn't want to save me either. It

needs me. It craves for me. And to it, my sex is deep and sacred, deeper than I am, with a deep nature aware deep down of my sex. It saves me from cheapness, mother. And even you could never do that for me."

Mrs. Witt rose to her feet, and stood looking far, far away, at the turquoise ridge of mountains half sunk under the horizon.

"How much did you say you paid for Las Chivas?" she asked.

"Twelve hundred dollars," said Lou, surprised.

"Then I call it cheap, considering all there is to it: even the name."

Mrs. Witt's deflationary remark is occasioned by her perception of the floundering repetitiveness, the schoolgirl vagueness by which Lou expresses a yearning which Lawrence in any case wants us to recognize as a commonplace of American literature. By now the reader compassionately knows that the failings in Lou's speech are a sign of her heroic struggle, in which Lawrence shares, for "verbal consciousness." Her verbal situation is made explicit in an earlier passage describing Mrs. Witt's:

The visible world, and the invisible. Or rather, the audible and the inaudible. She had lived so long, and so completely, in the visible, audible world. She would not easily admit that other, inaudible. She always wanted to jeer, as she approached the brink of it.

At a similar "brink," Lou refuses to become merely the social satirist; she takes the risk of showing herself vulnerable and entrapped, as under the circumstances she must be. Like the New England woman and like other heroes of her nationality, she is trying to do something in itself impossible: to live only within the freedom of that reality which her own consciousness has created:

> And if it had been a question simply of living through the eyes, into the *distance,* then this would have been Paradise, and the little New England woman on her ranch would have found what she was always looking for, the earthly paradise of the spirit.
>
> But even a woman cannot live only into the distance, the beyond. Willy-nilly she finds herself juxtaposed to the near things, the thing in itself. And willy-nilly she is caught up into the fight with the immediate object.

The impossibility of living through the "eye" is the impossibility of totally divorcing the self from time, biology, economics, and the words by which the free, visionary environment of the "eye" is translated into that social entity: the "I," living in relation to "near things." Lawrence here recognizes that Lou's dilemma for anyone determined to make it the subject of literature, imposes nearly insuperable problems of expression. The recognition is not itself an accomplishment. Emerson had long before articulated it in "The Poet" and "The Transcendentalist." What distinguishes Lawrence is his refusal to evade in his writing the difficulties of which he is also a theoretician. Only a few American writers, similarly concerned with the invisible and inaudible world, deserve, as the next chapter tries to show, to be so honored.

# II

## Is There an I for an Eye?:
## The Visionary Possession of America

"America is a poem in our eyes."
EMERSON

There is no better illustration of the Laurentian conflict, the "struggle," again, "for verbal consciousness," than in those oddly frequent passages in the classics of American literature where the hero becomes in effect a version of Emerson's "transparent eyeball": the hero's relationships, like those of Lou Witt in *St. Mawr*, devolve, that is, entirely to his vision. Where these scenes occur in American literature, they are, unlike the last scene of *St. Mawr*, almost invariably and exclusively descriptive. Devoid of bodily movement or dialogue, they have the form of soliloquy. Necessarily so: the eye cannot speak, it can only enlarge itself as it takes in the world, and if it is to do so with maximum autonomy, the rest of the body and its functions must be surrendered to it. "The eye," writes Emerson, "is the best of artists," and in part he meant that even while it encircles infinitely larger areas and discovers an incomparably greater variety of relationships than do other bodily instruments, it remains marvelously unencumbered. It can pick up things or drop them, join them or separate them, love them or hate them — all without let or hindrance. By nature, the eye is the freest, most gregarious, most omniverous of organs; and because its freedom is at one with its nature it qualifies as the "best of artists" in Emerson's sense.

But in fact no artist is so free as an eyeball, no one can live or write, or, in Henry James Sr.'s definition of possible Artists, wait on table only with the eyes. Hence this question: how, from the images of a visionary or aesthetic relationship to the world, can we extrapolate the actions and dialogues, the involvements and relationships that are the inescapable demand made by literature, notably by fiction? To take possession of America in the eye, as an Artist, is a way of preserving imaginatively those dreams about the continent that were systematically betrayed by the possession of it for economic and political aggrandizement. A competing, more practical and realistic act of possession involved the imagined rape of the virgin land, and to those who felt like impotent witnesses, the concept of the Artist or "poet" affirmed a possibly noble role in the drama of national conquest. Considering the odd configurations by which the different kinds of possession get into play, the possessive eye operating at the expense of possessive hands, it is possible to think that even the word "continent" might have caused American writers some uneasiness. One meaning of the word is "to contain," and the "poet" like America itself was supposed to contain multitudes in harmony; but the word also means "self-restraint" or "abstinence," especially in sexual activity. It is not an idle pun that the men in American literature who visually possess the continent or even, like James's Strether, a distillation of two continents, are often themselves "continent."

A book that expresses these ideas with an acknowledg-
ment of their sexual implications found scarcely
anywhere else in American literature is *The Great
Gatsby*. For good reason, everyone remembers the striking passage at the end about the "green light, the
orgiastic future," a section of the book that Fitzgerald
wisely decided to move from an earlier part so that it
might be a coda for the whole. As Nick sees it, the
"green light" at the end of the Buchanan's dock is a
modern version of what "flowered once for Dutch sailors' eyes — a fresh, green breast of the new world . . .
the last and greatest of all human dreams." Imagining
the position of the earliest visitors to the shore on which
he stands, he feels that "for a transitory, enchanted moment man must have held his breath in the presence of
this continent, compelled into an aesthetic contemplation he neither understood nor desired, face to face for
the last time in history with something commensurate to
his capacity for wonder."

The passage illustrates those qualities that make Fitzgerald appealing both as a person and as a writer: the
risks he takes for his characters, his generosity of feeling
for those who must express their ideals meretriciously,
his reticence in situations where other writers would be
eager to display their ironic awareness. In Fitzgerald,
that awareness is expressed as if the measure and restraint of his prose were at his own and not at his characters' expense. This aristocracy of manner is apparent,
too, in the unstrenuous particularity by which, even
while allowing nothing about his heroes to appear
merely shameful, he proliferates details that do have the
effect of discreetly placing his people, qualifying their
illusions and their efforts at self-expansion. For these

reasons, Fitzgerald's "man," gazing at the unspoiled
continent, simply cannot be equated with Crèvecoeur's
"new man" — a vulgar and silly conception. Instead,
even while evoking that figure, he is also sensibly com-
paring him to sailors at the end of a long voyage from
Europe, thereby giving a very human substance to the
remark that "aesthetic contemplation," however instinctive to the eye under such circumstances, will necessarily
be at odds (it is "compelled," it is "neither understood
nor desired") with the rewards actually desired of the
landscape. Imposing a further realistic restraint is the
fact that Nick's evocation of a historical vision of America occurs at a time and at a place — not far from the ash
heaps of Long Island — when, as the novel itself has
been showing, the continent is possessed and exploited
in a way that makes any "asethetic contemplation" not
merely nostalgic, but perhaps a recourse from an admission of impotence.

Such discriminations about the visionary ideal of
America would be commonplace in most other writers,
but in Fitzgerald they are unobtrusively localized within the sexual failures — the "orgiastic future" is exactly
right — which the novel records. If the continent as a
"green breast" has been violated since that day when it
"flowered once for Dutch sailors' eyes," so has Daisy
since that magical and equally transitory moment when,
at the touch of Gatsby's lips, she "blossomed for him
like a flower, and the incantation was complete."

Fitzgerald shares with Dreiser a genius for imagining
sex as a function of some larger vision that is elsewhere
in American literature anxiously divorced from it. Fitzgerald does not separate dreams of the Platonic from the
sexual self, and like Dreiser he makes a story out of the

difficulties that sex interposes in any fantasy of an
autonomously expanding self. A corresponding inter-
position of sex between the self and its visionary goals is
rare in American literature, occurring not at all in
Emerson or Thoreau, very weakly in Melville except in
*Pierre*, in Hawthorne only by way of sermonizing
against it, and in James usually with a very elaborate
machinery for disposing of it. In this regard, John Jay
Chapman, whose essay on Emerson remains one of the
best things written about him and the phenomenon he
represents, observed that "If an inhabitant of another
planet should visit the earth, he would receive, on the
whole, a truer notion of life by attending an Italian
opera than he would by reading Emerson's volumes. He
would learn from the Italian opera that there were two
sexes; and this, after all, is probably the fact with which
the education of a stranger ought to begin." To which it
should immediately be added that if the stranger then
wanted to learn why Italian opera isn't the only thing
one listens to he could in Emerson discover those wild-
est of all hopes for a kind of self-expansion that exceeds
anything even in the Italian opera. When Emerson does
allude to artificial life, it is to find buried there the
startling, strange, barbaric life of nature:

> We talk of deviations from natural life, as if
> artificial life were not also natural. The
> smoothest curled courtier in the boudoirs of a
> palace has an animal nature, rude and aborigi-
> nal as a white bear, omnipotent to its own
> ends, and is directly related, there amid essen-
> ces and billets doux, to Himmaleh mountain-
> chains and the axis of the globe.

Given this anticipation, pointed out to me by Anita Van Vactor, of the most mysterious aspects of the later James, who is to say what Emerson's style could *not* embrace?

To consider Fitzgerald in conjunction with Emerson, is to recognize Fitzgerald's consistent daring and intelligence working in the direction of this passage from the shorter essay "Nature." While Emerson was aware of what he called our "double consciousness" — our commitment at one moment to a dream of the self and at another to immediate profit in the "buzz and din" of ordinary life — he sought by his images to extend our consciousness so that it would be beyond but inclusive of the polarities of this doubleness. But for Fitzgerald, the tension could not be so ameliorated, one aspect of reality being forced, always unsuccessfully, to serve or represent the other. Never afraid of the difficulty of exposing the ridiculousness of vision by emphasizing the gap between it and reality, he could write the famous scene where Gatsby piles his beautiful shirts in front of Daisy and Nick. These shirts, according to Marius Bewley, are "sacramental" and are brought forth with a "reverential humility in the presence of some inner vision he cannot consciously grasp." Mr. Bewley is surely right in saying that the incident does not, as some have claimed, show Fitzgerald's failure of critical control of values. And yet the word "sacramental" puts perhaps too much of a burden on this pathetic moment; that it barely comes off at all is precisely its significance. It enacts the necessarily clumsy effort to connect a vision of what is to be possessed with what one can actually show for it.

There are, of course, parallels to this problem in English romantic poetry. But it is only in American literature that such visions are a repeated preoccupation of prose fiction. This is a fact of crucial significance. Prose, and especially prose fiction, to an extent not observable in poetry, necessarily confronts any effort at an "aesthetic contemplation" whether of women or of property with embarrassing practical, social, and biological questions. *The Great Gatsby* is an important work not because it evokes certain mythologies that are recurrent in American literature. Its distinction is in its unusual awareness of some of the problems besetting that literature: how can these mythologies be sustained, it asks, in the face of the practical considerations which novels, as much as our social and biological history, insist upon?

With these problems of expression in mind, we should, of course, begin any anthology of the theme of visionary possession in American literature with Emerson. Even though he doesn't initiate it, as we learn from Perry Miller's *Errand Into the Wilderness,* he gave it life and flamboyance; it was he who generated it into literary mythology. Indeed, so powerful has Emerson been that his works now constitute a compendium of iconographies that have gotten into American writers who may never have liked or even read him. He is found in Faulkner, who probably looked at his writings in school, as much as in Cooper, who had little taste for the little he knew of him, in Mark Twain who smirked at him, in James who patronizingly admired him, in Frost who worshipped him, and in Wallace Stevens who, in his elegant turn toward European literature, seemed rather shy of admitting those similarities between himself and Emerson which have been recently defined by Harold Bloom. To consider the opening of "Nature" with only the closing of *The Great Gatsby* for comparison is to recognize a confluence of metaphors the

more remarkable for being unpremediated, and to
know that the themes announced by these metaphors
belong to American literature through agencies more
mysterious than direct literary influence:

> To go into solitude, a man needs to retire
> as much from his chamber as from society.
> I am not solitary whilst I read and write,
> though nobody is with me. But if a man would
> be alone, let him look at the stars. The rays
> that come from those heavenly worlds will sep-
> arate between him and what he touches. One
> might think the atmosphere was made trans-
> parent with this design, to give man, in the
> heavenly bodies, the perpetual presence of the
> sublime. Seen in the streets of cities, how great
> they are! If the stars should appear one night
> in a thousand years, how would men believe
> and adore; and preserve for many generations
> the remembrance of the city of God which had
> been shown! But every night come out these
> envoys of beauty, and light the universe with
> their admonishing smile.
>
> The stars awaken a certain reverence, be-
> cause though always present, they are inacces-
> sible; but all natural objects make a kindred
> impression, when the mind is open to their in-
> fluence. Nature never wears a mean appear-
> ance. Neither does the wisest man extort her
> secret, and lose his curiosity by finding out all
> her perfection. Nature never became a toy to a
> wise spirit. The flowers, the animals, the
> mountains, reflected the wisdom of his best

hour, as much as they had delighted the simplicity of his childhood.

When we speak of nature in this manner, we
have a distinct but most poetical sense in the
mind. We mean the integrity of impression
made by manifold natural objects. It is this
which distinguishes the stick of timber of the
wood-cutter from the tree of the poet. The
charming landscape which I saw this morning
is indubitably made up of some twenty or
thirty farms. Miller owns this field, Locke that,
and Manning the woodland beyond. But none
of them owns the landscape. There is a property in the horizon which no man has but he
whose eye can integrate all the parts, that is,
the poet. This is the best part of these men's
farms, yet to this their warranty-deeds give no
title.

To speak truly, few adult persons can see nature. Most persons do not see the sun. At least
they have a very superficial seeing. The sun il-
luminates only the eye of the man, but shines
into the eye and heart of the child. The lover
of nature is he whose inward and outward
senses are still truly adjusted to each other;
who has retained the spirit of infancy even
into the era of manhood. His intercourse with
heaven and earth becomes part of his daily
food. In the presence of nature a wild delight
runs through the man, in spite of real sorrows.
Nature says — he is my creature, and maugre
all his impertinent griefs, he shall be glad with
me. Not the sun or the summer alone, but ev-

ery hour and season yields its tribute of delight; for every hour and change corresponds to and authorizes a different state of the mind, from breathless noon to grimmest midnight. Nature is a setting that fits equally well a comic or a mourning piece. In good health, the air is a cordial of incredible virtue. Crossing a bare common, in snow puddles, at twilight, under a clouded sky, without having in my thoughts any occurrence of special good fortune, I have enjoyed a perfect exhilaration. I am glad to the brink of fear. In the woods, too, a man casts off his years, as the snake his slough, and at what period soever of life is always a child. In the woods is perpetual youth. Within these plantations of God, a decorum and sanctity reign, a perennial festival is dressed, and the guest sees not how he should tire of them in a thousand years. In the woods, we return to reason and faith. There I feel that nothing can befall me in life, — no disgrace, no calamity (leaving me my eyes), which nature cannot repair. Standing on the bare ground, — my head bathed by the blithe air and uplifted into infinite space, — all mean egotism vanishes. I become a transparent eyeball; I am nothing; I see all; the currents of the Universal Being circulate through me; I am part or parcel of God. The name of the nearest friend sounds then foreign and accidental: to be brothers, to be acquaintances, master or servant, is then a trifle and a disturbance. I am the lover of uncontained and immortal beauty. In

the wilderness, I find something more dear and
connate than in streets or villages. In the tran-
quil landscape, and especially in the distant
line of the horizon, man beholds somewhat as
beautiful as his own nature.

The greatest delight which the fields and
woods minister is the suggestion of an occult
relation between man and the vegetable. I am
not alone and unacknowledged. They nod to
me, and I to them. The waving of the boughs
in the storm is new to me and old. It takes me
by surprise, and yet is not unknown. Its effect
is like that of a higher thought or a better
emotion coming over me, when I deemed I
was thinking justly or doing right.

Yet it is certain that the power to produce
this delight does not reside in nature, but in
man, or in a harmony of both. It is necessary to
use these pleasures with great temperance. For
nature is not always tricked in holiday attire,
but the same scene which yesterday breathed
perfume and glittered as for the frolic of the
nymphs is overspread with melancholy to-day.
Nature always wears the colors of the spirit.
To a man laboring under calamity, the heat of
his own fire hath sadness in it. Then there is a
kind of contempt of the landscape felt by him
who has just lost by death a dear friend. The
sky is less grand as it shuts down over less
worth in the population.

This first section of "Nature," is familiar to everyone,
mostly because of the image of the "transparent eye-

ball." During the four paragraphs preceding this image, the speaker might also be recognized as a version of the sailors who — some eighty-five years later — will share a vision of the unviolated landscape of America with Nick Carroway. Both in Emerson and in Fitzgerald relation to landscape is established by gazing at it, by an "aesthetic contemplation" rather than by more palpable and profitable claims to ownership. When Nick looks at the shore line, "the inessential houses began to melt away," a preliminary to his own loss of identifying form, so that he himself becomes timeless and mythologized, a participant in the prospects that "must have flowered once for Dutch sailors' eyes." These houses on Long Island are like the farms that in the third paragraph of "Nature" set boundaries in the landscape, farms that also "melt" or decompose as a prelude to the speaker's own liberation from the boundaries of self and time. Disintegration of fabricated forms like houses and boundaries is the precondition both in Fitzgerald and in Emerson for a new integration that occurs in the contemplative-aesthetic-poetic eye.

To use verbs of seeing and possessing in the manner of Emerson is to be necessarily satiric of the way these words are used by the society alluded to at the beginning of the passage in his references to farm owners or to "most persons" who "do not see" things properly, who cannot "see nature." Significantly, the opening sentence subordinates the speaker's separation from society to his withdrawal from the "study" — "to go into solitude, a man needs to retire as much from his chamber as from society." He cannot be alone, that is, when he reads or writes because books and the use of language connect him with civilization which, like society, has been systematized. He is, in effect, separating himself from language because it draws its meaning not only from socially accepted usage but from literature itself.

A roughly similar act of separation is implicit in the passage from Fitzgerald: the Dutch sailors have left the Old World of social system and storied civilization to face a wilderness, while Nick has turned his back literally and figuratively on the society of East and West Egg, sitting alone on the shore to brood about Gatsby's and America's dreams. This act of separation, this relinquishment of social and literary ties, is the final evidence in American literature that a man is becoming a "poet," finding his proper "style." But again, the recurrence of such a paradigm is less important than its particular manifestations. The point has already been made that these images of separation do not characteristically take on significance within a dramatic relationship involving the hero with elements of society. They get expressed instead in his soliloquies, in his communions with landscape for which he has rejected social conversation. Instances occur in almost any of the American classics with great variety of intensity and effect. And yet it is obvious that Fitzgerald's investment in this sequence is not at all so heavy as Emerson's. Unlike Emerson or Thoreau, unlike Cooper or even Henry James, Fitzgerald has no *a priori* commitment to the renunciation of social ties, or to the visionary advantages that derive from it. He is rather a worried participant in the custom by which the heroes of American literature are allowed to turn their backs on the ways and wiles of systematic society in order that they may enter what Emerson calls "an original relation to the universe."

Precisely because Emerson was anxious to make us believe in the integrity and at least momentary autonomy of visionary experience, and because he did not want to adulterate this experience by mixing it with mundane and incompatible requirements of life, Emerson can be said to have taken on a more difficult task in his writing than does Fitzgerald. In "Nature" and in his work generally, he tries to make the ideals of relinquishment and visionary possession not a rationale of conduct so much as its actual, its conscious substance. Yet, Emerson, most attractively, feared being left merely to "the splendid labyrinth of my perceptions," of "balking ordinary affections by denying substantive life to men and women." Hence his manner of writing involves him continually in rationalizing, even seeming to apologize by his tone for the revolutionary sentiments that he is meanwhile asserting.

Henry Nash Smith points, I think, to one of the most interesting aspects of Emerson when he refers to "Emerson's problem of vocation." Implicit in his rejection of "society" was a rejection of the roles which it honored and rewarded. Having abandoned the ministry in 1832, having found no satisfactory substitute for it either in the strongly acquisitive business society of Boston during that decade or in the groups of reformers in the next who, like those at Brook Farm, surrendered to yet another kind of institutionalized action, Emerson invented the ideal type of self-expressive man who supplies the titles of some of his essays — The Scholar, Representative Men, The Poet. Being a poet in the sense that he defines one, being, that is, a man who can relinquish the accouterments of society and civilization in order to possess a purer and larger sense of the self — this represents a touching solution to his "problem of vocation." The "transparent eyeball" is itself an imaginary role, a version of "the poet," to which he attempts to give a greater reality than that belonging to the roles he rejects. Obviously, the eyeball as possessor is an imaginative analogue to the great American enterprise of the period. To a man of the early nineteenth century in America, possessing landscape was necessarily more than a romantic commonplace of descriptive-reflective poetry. Possession was also a national goal entrusted to enterprising men who faced an opportunity for profit unique in history.

The position in which Emerson found himself should engage the same appreciation given nowadays to the situation of artists at a time closer in spirit to our own, of the *fin de siècle* as represented in, say, Pater, or in Joyce's "portrait" of a Pateresque artist. What was left to Emerson was the task of imagining a role for himself not merely as a writer. He had literally to enact the role *in* his writing. Only here could he be the "poet" he imagines. Rejecting as explicitly as he does all institutionalized allegiances, he is forced to claim a place and function for himself almost wholly through his style. His function could not come to life outside his pages since he is explicitly disdainful of the idea that absorbs the attention of Fitzgerald and James: that the idealized self can function in terms of the world of social and economic systems.

To put such a burden on style is not uncharacteristic of American writers, especially of Melville, James, or Faulkner. To do so while writing in the polite forms and styles of Emerson's essays, however, is sometimes to miscalculate the burden. He had a distaste for fiction and thus for a form in which he could have had a multitude of voices strengthening his own by manipulated contrasts. Such a technique is obviously indispensable to the novelists just mentioned, to James, say, in convincing us of the virtues of Isabel or Strether, to Melville in revealing the heroism of Ahab. Emerson was primarily an essayist and lecturer, seldom choosing to argue alternative positions within a given piece, and he writes the same way, uses the same style for all aspects of experience. His personal letters are in this respect no different from his public speeches. His unalterable consistency of tone, except in rare instances like the essay "Experience," is perhaps one reason why he *sounds* rather simple to modern readers. But evidence that he was theoretically aware of the difficulties of his situation and of the literary problems it involved is abundant, as in "The Transcendentalist," where he gives his account of our "double consciousness," or in his characterization of the only momentary successes of the poet who seems to "be free" and to "make free" only in his tropes, or in his lamentation in "Experience" that grief itself has no reality for him. The latter essay is nearly an admission that Emerson's renowned indifference to evil might be charged as much to emotional shallowness as to philosophical conviction.

Emerson's theories and recognitions must not, however, be confused with his performances. In his performances, his structuring of sentences and paragraphs, especially in so early an effort as "Nature," he often unwittingly evades the struggle with language to which those causes would seem necessarily to commit him. His style, by which I mean his projected presence in the rhythms and vocabularies of his prose, often reveals a subjection, even an allegiance to the very forms and conventions which are at the same time being attacked. The pictorialized elements in the opening of "Nature," for example, are not wholly coherent with the audible ones. There is no speaking "I" for the seeing "eye." Or to put it another way, the romantic images of relinquishment and possession get entrapped within the social environment created in the speaker's address to his readers.

Of course, if we forget about voice, and consider the passage rather mechanically only as an extended metaphor about sight, then the opening of "Nature" would be demonstrably coherent. In this respect, the passage shows every evidence of Emerson's metaphoric power exerting itself to authenticate an incredible moment of self-transformation. The moment occurs when, "Standing on the bare ground, — my head bathed by the blithe air and uplifted into infinite space, — all mean egotism vanishes. I become a transparent eyeball; I am nothing; I see all; the currents of the Universal Being circulate through me; I am part or parcel of God. The name of the nearest friend sounds then foreign and accidental: to be brothers, to be acquaintances, master or servant, is then a trifle and a disturbance." The many variations on ideas of seeing and transparency in the preceding paragraphs of "Nature" do indeed condition us to welcome the "transparent eyeball" when it appears. The narrator's transformation is further anticipated by his curious changes and expansions of identity throughout the opening of the essay, especially in his use of pronouns. The opening sentence is general and aphoristic ("a man needs to retire"), the next is more emphatically personal ("I am not solitary whilst I read and write"). The shifts continue: from "a man" to "I" to "one" simply to "man" as subjects of the verbs, and throughout the remainder of the passage there are similar shifts — to "we" back to "I" to "most persons" to "man" to "I" and so forth, even though he is usually talking about his own uniquely quasi-mystical relation to things. Thus, even in the grammar we experience the speaker's capacity to relinquish his particular identity and assume an ever more inclusively general one. In addition, he shifts into tones of voice and into vocabularies reserved for the different vocations that deal professionally with the relation between men and landscape — terms that belong to the surveyor, the farmer, the philosopher, the aesthetician. He mixes these voices and vocabularies with a self-confident ease, thereby sounding like a composite man before he explicitly claims to be one. The reader comes to accept a man so multiple, so general, so inclusive as to be in effect a "transparent eyeball," seeing everything and letting us see everything in him, long before he actually claims to be one. So that there is plenty of evidence in the passage of Emerson trying to transport us from the society of "joint stock companies" — where the landscape belongs to Miller, Locke, and Manning, who own its farms — to the world of Emerson's imagining, where such ownership is relinquished so that the Self may be possessed by and come into possession of the cosmos.

The writing is, in the manipulation of metaphors, a stunning example of Emerson's genius. But if we listen to the passage rather than merely work out patterns of metaphor, if we ask ourselves not what is revealed by analysis of images but what is experienced by our being alert to the sound of the voice addressing us, we cannot

then say that Emerson as "transparent eyeball" has
managed to displace Miller, Locke, and Manning as
owners of the landscape or as proprietors of reality.
Emerson's opposition to conventional systems prevents
his appealing for support to any realities constituted
outside his own language. And yet Emerson's tone in
the opening of "Nature" seldom manages to be more
than compliantly evocative of the social forms it wants
us to disown. Even in the few passages already quoted,
the reader is made to feel in a relation less to a revolutionary than to an urbane, highly literary, even rather
clubbable man. To speak of withdrawal with the elegant presumptuousness of the opening sentence — "To
go into solitude, a man needs to retire as much from his
chamber as from society" — may invite all of us into the
woods but will it offend anyone who stays in the drawing room? He sounds as if he were planning a trip to the
country not with Wordsworth but with Addison and
Steele. A man who says that the stars "light the Universe
with their admonishing smile" and who refers to "the
charming landscape which I saw this morning" is using
phrases that domesticate both himself and nature,
phrases of a genteei good taste that necessarily moder-
ates our response to the later hyperbolic definition of his
relation, as a "transparent eyeball," to nature, to society,
and to the reader. Even the direct criticisms made in the
passage, such as the remark that "to speak truly few
adults can see nature," defers to polite sentimentalities
about *really* seeing things, and leaves to speculation the
meaning of "nature" itself. The energy expended here,
and the corresponding energy elicited from the reader
are conspicuously insufficient to Emerson's intentions.
Indeed we recognize the ambitions of this passage only

by sensing that there is something askew in its style. By
contrast we might recall Thoreau's very vigorous activity in sentences where he wants the reader's active assent
to his claims that "I retained the landscape and . . .
annually carted off what it yielded without a wheel bar-
row." Emerson in this and many other instances is victim of what Santayana calls the "kindly infidelities of
language," its tendency to "vitiate the experience it expresses."

Emerson in many respects *is* American literature,
both by virtue of the themes and images of which he is
its storehouse and because of the exciting ways in which
the impossible ambitions he has for his writing often
fail, but only just barely, of being realized. Thus his
style in this passage, admittedly an early one, tends to
make his ideas of relinquishment and possession seem
safe and respectable — an anticipation of what happens
to Mark Twain in *Huckleberry Finn* — despite the necessities of his personal position. "Emerson had his mes-
sage," James the novelist wisely observed, "but he was a
good while looking for his form." And in this difficulty
he is the exemplum of those American writers, to me
the most interesting, who cannot hide their dissatisfaction and their resultant struggle with the forms and
styles they are using.

Again, though by now it should be apparent, my interest is not in tracing in American literature images of
the poetic eye and attendant images of relinquishment
and possession. I am concerned rather with the condition of these images within the environments created by
particular works or passages. Obviously the only possible environment for them is in a context invented by
the writer, the initial proposition being that they are

only antagonistically received, if indeed they aren't ob-
literated, in the real world, or in literature which allows
itself to be merely a mirror of that world. The results of
my emphasis will, I hope, reveal something about history as well as about literature: it should let us measure
the degree of conflict between assumptions of reality
embedded in the conventions of literary expression, as
against the often antagonistic assumptions implicit in
certain images of American romantic idealism. American writers show a noticeable difficulty both in escaping
those conventions of expression and in creating a stylistic environment that will be hospitable to the "poet"
enacting the drama of relinquishment and possession.
When Emerson remarks in his *Journals* that the two
barriers to literary and intellectual accomplishment in
America are "our devotion to property" and the "influence of Europe," he reveals an intuitive grasp of how
efforts to dispel the first are inseparable from the literary problems posed by the second. In trying to modify
"our devotion to property" it was necessary profoundly
to modify the literary conventions, especially of prose,
that constrain or even direct our consciousness of the
self and of reality.

The American preoccupation with varieties of possession has a special poignancy when we think of our writers' articulating an idealized "poetic" claim to a new
world but in ways indicating that the old one is still in
"possession" of their literary means. In a way I am only
repeating the familiar perception of Robert Frost in
"The Gift Outright." Even after the separation from
England, our greatest national effort at relinquishment,
we could not "possess" America, so the poem goes, because our imaginations were for a time still "Possessed

by what we now no more possessed": England. Whitman had a similarly phrased complaint in 1871, asking that we "entirely recast the types of highest personality from what the oriental, feudal, ecclesiastical worlds bequeath us, and which yet possess the imaginative and aesthetic fields of the United States."

We might suppose that Cooper's Deerslayer, a great renouncer of "property," and of "devotion to Europe," would adequately represent Whitman's type of "highest personality." However, Whitman is not talking about ideas and mythic intentions; deeply serious writer that he was, he is concerned with the literary performance needed to articulate them. His concern is for the "casting" of character and the effort therein to escape from the inherited models derived from the "feudal" world. Measured by such a standard, Cooper is extremely vulnerable to criticisms, especially those made by Mark Twain, the antagonist, along with Whitman, of the genteel literary traditions of which he was also a victim. Mark Twain's essay on the literary offenses of Cooper's novels is usually dismissed as a good joke, or, in the words of a recent partisan of Cooper, as the reaction of "an embittered realist against romanticism at its height in prose fiction." Mark Twain is not complaining only about romanticism, however, but mostly about Cooper's laziness, an aspect of which is his apathetic mingling, in his hero's dialogue, of a semi-literate vernacular, of which the author is needlessly proud, with a pretentiously literary phraseology about which he ought to be embarrassed. When we think of the Leather-Stocking Tales years after reading them we forget the hero's dialogue and remember him as one of the great creations of American fiction. It is on record that Deerslayer means a great deal to many people, convincing proof that books do work mysteriously, making a composite appeal to the reader's fascination for certain images, a fascination so deep that perhaps it doesn't matter that so far as he can be said to exist by his conversation the hero is a bore. Deerslayer is in the truest sense a mythic character, and he deserves to be, not for his mouthings of virtue and of ideas that belong to the history of ideas, but for his being the incarnation of the American *"beau ideal"*: silent, marvelously alert, capable of irresistible mechanical proficiency without explanatory claptrap, the servant of principles the more eloquent for being vaguely defined, and with a will undisrupted by muddled personal feelings of sexual love or the desire for gain. This is the Deerslayer a contemporary reader could find interesting, not the Sunday School prize essayist who emerges from the dialogue.

But the dialogue unfortunately exists. So does the evident need of the author to bring his hero into conventional novelistic situations, demonstrating thereby that he has not forgotten what life in English novels is all about. At such points we do not need to remind ourselves of the home truth that a myth, even a "yearning" one, as Lawrence describes Cooper's, is as effective as the style that creates it. However much Deerslayer appeals to us in the accounts of his actions and of his silent communication with landscape, it is equally revealing to consider Cooper's effort to give him life as it is traditionally given to characters in novels — a social life, defined by his speech and by his dramatized relationships to other people. Here again we witness the attempt to find a social voice for an anti-social, essentially inhuman embodiment of the American "poet" in the acts of relinquishment and possession.

Deerslayer is more capable and slick than anyone he meets, not only Indians but also other guides and settlers. So that his failure in practical terms — he owns nothing and takes no woman as wife or lover — has the effect of making the successful acquisitiveness of those less capable than he seem short-sighted and contemptible. "Now here am I, a hunter and a scout, and a guide," he observes near the end of *The Pathfinder,* "although I do not own a foot of land on 'arth, yet do I enjoy and possess more than the great Albany Patroon" (meaning Van Rensselaer). Deerslayer is one of the breed honored by Parkman as well as by Cooper, pioneers of the American wilderness who dispossess the savages in order to claim the land for a civilization that will in turn dispossess and crush them. Deerslayer himself owns the land only as a guide owns it, in his mind and by his vision. *The Pathfinder* begins with four people gazing at the wilderness and the assurance that "The sublimity connected with vastness is familiar to every eye," while in the opening of *The Deerslayer* the hero is described "gazing at the view which so much delighted him . . . the deep repose — the solitudes, that spoke of scenes and forests untouched by the hands of man."

Along with similarly evoked figures in American literature, Deerslayer is said at this moment of solitary contemplation to feel, "though it was unconsciously, like a poet also." He is still another version of Emerson's poet, joining the "aesthetic contemplation" of Fitzgerald's sailors, or the Thoreau who tills the bean field for the "sake of tropes and expression," or James's Strether

on his journey, at the crisis of *The Ambassadors,* alone
into the French countryside to find in landscape the
equivalent of a little painting by Lambinet. He is also an
early version of Isaac McCaslin in Faulkner's *The Bear,*
whose experiences are explained by his cousin with quo-
tations from Keats's "Ode on a Grecian Urn." The consistency of the "poet" figure is something to marvel at, a
confirmation that we are witness to a phenomenon in the
imagination of American writers that forces its way into
very different works even where it can expect little hos-
pitality.

"A magnificent moral hermaphrodite" is what Balzac
calls Deerslayer, and he is hermaphroditic in more than
a moral sense. In the three concluding chapters of *The
Pathfinder,* following his claim to possess more than the
Albany Patroon even though he owns nothing, Deerslayer agrees to surrender his claims not only to land but
to the woman he loves, Mable Dunham. He turns her
over to his friend Jaspar with the patronizingly humble
admission that "you will make her happier than I could,
for your gifts are better suited to do so." At this point
Cooper slips into an unconscious revelation of the peculiar role assigned his hero in the advance of civilization. Faced with Deerslayer's sacrifice, "Jaspar and
Mable sat," we are told, "resembling Milton's picture of
our first parents, when consciousness of sin first layed its
leaden weight on their souls." Their future does indeed
depend on Deerslayer's wanting, like James's Strether,
nothing for himself. He offers here an example of that
redemptive sacrifice for human history which some
American writers discover not only in their heroes, but
also in their own function as artists in American society.
Emerson comes close on several occasions to speaking of

himself as Christ, and of course there are numerous fictional versions, like Isaac McCaslin, who consciously emulate the Nazarene (and Deerslayer) in rejecting profit and married life.

Discovering Christ figures in American literature is still accounted an achievement even though it takes some dexterity to avoid them. The only thing worth noticing about the recurrence is that most American writers are much more skeptical about them than are archetypal critics. No such critical skepticism is at work, however, in those parts of the Leather-Stocking Tales where Deerslayer is shown as a Christ-like victim. Because of such abatement of critical control, features of his character meant to seem divine are allowed also, and with no extended enrichment, to seem hermaphroditic, priggish, or latently homosexual. What can one do — or rather what one can not do — with Deerslayer's assurance to Jaspar that "if I had to marry you, boy, I should give myself no consarn about being well looked upon, for you have always shown a disposition to see me and all I do with a friendly eye. But a young gal, after all, must wish to marry a man that is nearer her own age and fancies." Again, the suggestion is that it is somehow superior to appreciate things in a "friendly eye" rather than by the sort of physical possession ruled out by his deprecating comments on age and a gal's fancy.

Cooper is remarkably innocent here in what he suggests about his hero; and he is unpardonably slack in protecting him from the sexual definitions that Mr. Fiedler is prepared to make. Embarrassments of this kind occur whenever there is an effort to rationalize in social terms the romantic and religious ideals of the self represented by this kind of hero. Cooper was best in dealing with those elements of civilization that can be projected into the activity of scoundrels and cut-throats; his hero comes most brilliantly to life while contesting for possession of Glimmerglass with old Hutter, who embodies the forces of economic exploitation and who has literally claimed the lake as his own. Where *The Deerslayer* fails is at moments when the hero is made to express his worth within social situations made familiar by the novel of manners — in most scenes, for instance, with Hutter's stepdaughter Judith. She represents an element of civilization that looks to the social life of the local English garrison and treasures the frills of costume that belonged to her mother and fill what is essentially the daughter's hope chest. Despite her goodness of heart and her admiration for the hero's virtues, she conducts herself like a refugee from the novels of Jane Austen or, even more, of Thackeray or Scott. It is an impressive illustration of Cooper's moral feeling for literary types that at the end Judith, like Hawthorne's Pearl, is consigned a destiny phrased in the stock romance of a good number of English novels: "an old sergeant of the garrison, who had lately come from England, was enabled to tell our hero that Sir Robert Warley lived on his paternal estates, and that there was a lady of rare beauty in the lodge, who had great influence over him though she did not bear his name." Cooper can discover no way to bring about her necessary confrontation with Deerslayer without making the hero sound ridiculous, even though it is she who is supposed to seem unworthy. At his most impressive, Deerslayer is a character described rather than self-articulated, a man seen by the narrator "communing . . . without the aids of forms or language" rather than a conversationalist who, when asked by this young woman if he has a sweetheart, replies with the information that "She's in the forest, Judith — hanging from the boughs of the trees, in a soft rain — in the dew of the open grass . . . the sweet springs where I slake my thirst."

One can admire other American writers more stylistically anxious than Emerson or Cooper without therefore preferring them. Other writers, like Thoreau, Melville, Mark Twain, James, and Faulkner, acknowledge how difficult it is to give authority to ideas, specifically those of the "poet" as the hero of relinquishment and possession, which are otherwise defenseless against the claims of conventional reality. Of course, any such comparative evaluations are tentative: one kind of accomplishment in literature is not all accomplishments, and in this instance Emerson and Cooper probably could have done fewer of the things they do so superbly had they been more stylistically defensive. Nonetheless, these other writers show greater willingness to make the investment by which a protective environment can be created for some of the images and themes they share with Emerson. In the complications of their language and in their structural ingenuities, they force the reader actually to participate in "the struggle for verbal consciousness" that is to liberate us from customary suppositions about the meaning of words like "possession" or "nature," "the poet" or "reality." Their best performances are known for their intricacy, their opaqueness, even to the point where they are discussed not as books but as "problems for interpretation."

The reason for this degree of complexity, the reason, too, why so many of these works are read so badly, is that they require not that we bring to them the same kind of

awareness, even in a heightened form, that we bring to,
say, most English novels of the nineteenth century, but
that we submit to a discipline, imposed by the difficulties in the writing, that will develop in us a consciousness rarely called forth by English fiction before the
works of Hardy, E. M. Forster, and Lawrence, English
writers with an American penchant for moments of
heightened awareness in which characters step beyond
the boundaries of their daily environments. Ideally, the
result of such writing — all of *Moby-Dick* and *The Bear*
are conspicuous American illustrations — is the displacement of many of the reader's assumptions about
reality, and a change in our expectations about the
probable duration and sequence of events.

In *The Bear,* this effort to reshape the constituents of
reality is called "relinquishment," a word which also
describes Isaac's rejection of his inheritance and his
visionary possession of the wilderness. But before that it
refers, first, to a gutted log that is paradoxically said to
be "healing with unbelievable speed, a passionate and
almost visible relinquishment back into the earth";
later it describes how the boy surrenders to the wilderness and the bear by setting aside the instruments of
industrial power — gun, compass, and watch — so that
he "then relinquished completely to it"; and finally the
word describes Isaac's relationship to his inheritance
"not in pursuit and lust but in relinquishment." The
genius displayed is in Faulkner's effort of style; his style
makes "relinquishment" and "possession" a requirement
as much for the readers as for his hero. Consider, for
instance, the extraordinary use of negatives, almost from
the beginning of the story:

There was always a bottle present, so that it
would seem to him that those fine fierce in-
stants of heart and brain and courage and wili-
ness and speed were concentrated and distilled
into that brown liquor which not women, not
boys and children, but only hunters drank,
drinking not of the blood they spilled but
some condensation of the wild immortal spirit,
drinking it moderately, humbly even, not with
the pagan's base and baseless hope of acquiring
thereby the virtues of cunning and strength
and speed but in salute to them. Thus it
seemed to him on this December morning not
only natural but actually fitting that this
should have begun with whisky.

It is noticeable that the description of things being
dismissed by the negatives is never either foreshortened
or contemptuous. The tone and balance of attention are
deferential to those very aspects of reality that are being
at the same time discarded. One can feel here a strength
that is the essence of genius, a strength in having
reached a conviction about reality that may indeed deny
customary assumptions about its constituents but that is
never merely hateful or contemptuous of them. And in
any case the negatives do not apply merely to the practical view of a hunt; they apply just as energetically to
literary myths about hunting (as in the references to
drinking the "blood they spilled," or to the "pagan's
base and baseless hope") which the reader is apt to conjure up once he is assured that this hunt is not an
ordinary one.

Faulkner's style makes the reader's experience analogous to the hero's. The style requires that the reader divest himself of most of the conventional assumptions about hunting, people, and things that he brings to the story. At least Faulkner writes as if we do bring such assumptions to his work; that is precisely what makes him much more than a "Southern" novelist. He writes as if he could depend on very little public acceptance of the views he cherishes. Since Faulkner does acknowledge in the very grammar of refutation all that we might conventionally expect about the events he is narrating, his alternative version of them necessarily excites our attention and our consent. We experience thereby an unexpected extension of our consciousness of what such events might be. This sense of alternative possibilities is, in turn, located for us in the descriptive abstractions that pile up long before any object is attached to them. As we move through Faulkner's sentences we learn, having been denied expected supports, to grasp for those which *are* proffered, and these turn out to be the essentially visionary qualities of objects and accouterments associated with the hunt:

> He realised later that it had begun long before that. It had already begun on that day when he first wrote his age in two ciphers and his cousin McCaslin brought him for the first time to the camp, the big woods, to earn for himself from the wilderness the name and state of hunter provided he in his turn were humble and enduring enough. He had already inherited then, without ever having seen it, the big old bear with one trap-ruined foot that in an area al-

most a hundred miles square had earned for himself a name, a definite designation like a living man: — the long legend of corn-cribs broken down and rifled, of shoats and grown pigs and even calves carried bodily into the woods and devoured and traps and deadfalls overthrown and dogs mangled and slain and shotgun and even rifle shots delivered at point-blank range yet with no more effect than so many peas blown through a tube by a child — a corridor of wreckage and destruction beginning back before the boy was born, through which sped, not fast but rather with the ruthless and irresistible deliberation of a locomotive, the shaggy tremendous shape. It ran in his knowledge before he ever saw it. It loomed and towered in his dreams before he even saw the unaxed woods where it left its crooked print, shaggy, tremendous, red-eyed, not malevolent but just big, too big for the dogs which tried to bay it, for the horses which tried to ride it down, for the men and the bullets they fired into it; too big for the very country which was its constricting scope. It was as if the boy had already divined what his senses and intellect had not encompassed yet: that doomed wilderness whose edges were being constantly and punily gnawed at by men with plows and axes who feared it because it was wilderness, men myriad and nameless even to one another in the land where the old bear had earned a name, and through which ran not even a mortal beast but an anachronism in-

domitable and invincible out of an old dead
time, a phantom, epitome and apotheosis of
the old wild life which the little puny humans
swarmed and hacked at in a fury of abhorrence
and fear like pygmies about the ankles of a
drowsing elephant; — the old bear, solitary, in-
domitable, and alone; widowered childless and
absolved of mortality — old Priam reft of his
old wife and outlived all his sons.

Not merely the allusions at the end of this passage,
but the style itself suspends us in time. It saturates us in
a medium where objects are confused with the qualities
of objects or with the values attached to those objects, so
that "it" can refer to a cluster of impressions *about* the
bear, while the bear itself can be named mostly by various abstractions, legends, and allusions. By such writing
we are stripped, as Emerson wanted us to be, of dependable, conventional expectations, and our relation to reality is as open, mysterious, and expectant as that of
someone newborn. Precisely the same process is being
undergone by Isaac in these opening paragraphs. Faulkner's explicitness in this matter occurs, however, only
after we, like Isaac, have been made to feel it, to sense it
as inherent in the boy's experience and in the style
which renders it. This is a fact of considerable importance: the story both in its style and in its fable insists
that conceptions about experience derive from instincts
and confrontations, not the other way around:

He entered his novitiate to the true wilderness
with Sam beside him as he had begun his ap-
prenticeship in miniature to manhood after
the rabbits and such with Sam beside him, the

two of them wrapped in the damp, warm
negro-rank quilt while the wilderness closed
behind his entrance as it had opened momentarily to accept him, opening before his ad-
vancement as it closed behind his progress, no
fixed path the wagon followed but a channel
nonexistent ten yards ahead of it and ceasing
to exist ten yards after it had passed, the wagon
progressing not by its own volition but by attrition of their intact yet fluid circumambience, drowsing, earless, almost lightless.

The language here is an inducement to feel the
progress into the woods as a progress out of the womb
— the actual entrance into consciousness (from "fluid"
to something "almost lightless") evoking the passage of
the foetus into its first tentative groping toward the external world. But the woods are a second, not a first entrance into history for Isaac, and of course they are not
the initial entrance into history for us. They afford what
William James meant by "second birth," and Isaac's
progress in the woods thereafter prepares us for his later
relinquishment of inheritance and redefinition of his
place in history.

Faulkner, James, and Thoreau, in handling the
theme of possession, reveal their characteristic faith in
writing as an act of power, an act by which reality is
seized and dominated. In the works of each of them
style, as the previous chapter points out more generally,
is the final authority to which the reader may appeal for
verifications of reality. Of course each of them honors
something outside of style: in James it is often what he
means by "experience" ("Experience is never limited

and it is never complete"); in Faulkner what he calls "the things that touch the heart," a sort of atavism typically associated with notions of the organic community; and in Thoreau it is Nature in which he finds the creative agent. But if these powers are not wholly dependent for their existence upon the creative energy of the writer they are even more emphatically not dependent on any other kind of artifacts, other works of art or society, systems of any kind. The abstractions to which each of these writers feels subservient — "experience," "things that touch the heart," "nature" — are larger than any to which interpretive criticism can appeal. They refer us not to anything with a settled existence but rather to something of which the style itself is the synecdoche. The intense involvement in style required of the reader is notably strenuous in each of these writers, and there is always the temptation to escape from this involvement and to read the books as if they depended on more conventional social or psychological standards. These standards are often not so much irrelevant as below the mark in accounting for the extraordinary dislocations of our fixed ideas of reality that occur while we read James or Faulkner or Thoreau, the suspension and then the redirection of our way of seeing things and of feeling them through language. While James's later novels offer some conspicuous examples of the effects I describe, the evidence is of a kind that requires separate and highly qualified argument, and I prefer to conclude with the illustrative brevity allowed by Thoreau's *Walden*.

For all the attention paid to *Walden*, to its echoes of English literature of the seventeenth century, and to the author's capacity for word play, no one has sufficiently demonstrated its truly dazzling inventiveness and originality. As a fantasia of punning it is excelled only by *Finnegans Wake*. Its verbal play is designed to subvert the comfortable idioms that unite the communities of finance capitalism or of the "parlor," Thoreau's punning description of the place where words (parleying) are remote from the usages of the kitchen or of the out-of-doors. One of the best illustrations is a passage on the theme of relinquishment and possession that shows Thoreau's full awareness of the need actively to absorb, then to refashion, then to displace the commonly accepted meanings of words and idioms:

> At a certain season of our life we are accustomed to consider every spot as the possible site of a house. I have thus surveyed the country on every side within a dozen miles of where I live. In imagination I have bought all the farms in succession, for all were to be bought, and I knew their price. I walked over each farmer's premises, tasted his wild apples, discoursed on husbandry with him, took his farm at his price, at any price, mortgaging it to him in my mind; even put a higher price on it, — took everything but a deed of it, — took his word for his deed, for I dearly loved to talk, — cultivated it, and him too to some extent, I trust, and withdrew when I had enjoyed it long enough, leaving him to carry it on. This experience entitled me to be regarded as a sort of real-estate broker by my friends. Wherever I sat, there I might live, and the landscape radiated from me accordingly. What is a house but

a *sedes,* a seat? — better if a country seat. I discovered many a site for a house not likely to be
soon improved, which some might have
thought too far from the village, but to my
eyes the village was too far from it.

In any passage from Thoreau there is always a sentimental assumption that his reader automatically joins in
his sometimes coy discoveries of life's little ironies. The
phrase "for all were to be bought, and I knew their
price" is obviously meant to be devastating when it is in
fact tiresomely cute, and the repetition of "bought"
from the previous clause directs us not to any interesting root meaning of the term but only to the obvious
fact that he means it in a nonliteral sense. His language
sometimes asks us to pry and then yields nothing when
we do. Writing in this manner, Thoreau can be at once
flatfooted and arch. By contrast, his effective punning begins here with the remark that he "walked over each
farmer's premises." Characteristic of his best efforts, the
phrase does not anxiously call attention to itself, so that
for many readers it can pass, as indeed it seems to have
done, for what it most obviously says — that he walked
over the land owned by the farmers. Thoreau's best
jokes occur, however, precisely where he sounds most
harmless, most idiomatically familiar. Following on his
claim to possess all their farms in his imagination, the
phrase means that he "walks over" not only the land
they own but over the "premises" on which they base
their claims to ownership, the term referring in this
sense both to any proposition from which a conclusion is
drawn and also to the part of a deed or lease that states
the reasons for its being as it is.

Thoreau's genius with language, like Joyce's, is to an awesome degree self-satisfying. Both were apparently willing to go to the grave without having anyone recognize some of their best jokes, thereby confirming their theories about the condition of language in the societies about which each of them wrote. Having shown by the pun on the word "premises" how ordinary business usage can lull us to any but the most literal meanings of words, he then turns about and shows how we can miss such literal meanings because of the deadening familiarity of social idioms. Some such motive is at work, it seems, in the remainder of the sentence. Talking to the farmer about his land, he takes "everything but a deed of it, — took his word for his deed, for I dearly loved to talk, — cultivated it, and him too to some extent, I trust, and withdrew when I had enjoyed it long enough." The expression "I cultivated his friendship" is so familiar that we can be depended upon, almost, to miss the fact that in this context, where the word "cultivate" must also mean to till and improve land, Thoreau means not only that he makes friends with the farmer but that he improves him by his talk.* To improve the property owner by cultivating him means to make him part of the "cult" of owning land in the imagination, to make the farmer himself "walk over" his own "premises" about owning it in other ways. And a very reputable idiomatic phrase is then shown to contain a dangerous threat to those "premises" when Thoreau remarks that he "took his word for his deed," followed by a joke on the now obvious expensiveness of such conversation — "for I dearly loved to talk."

---

* Without intending a pun, Emerson wrote in "Self-Reliance" that a "cultivated man becomes ashamed of his property."

To be such a master of the inward richness of words is
to take visionary possession of the things to which the
words allude. In the manner of Donne, Thoreau includes all the ironies that might be directed against him,
turning them to his own profit, subject to his own
"premises." For these reasons he can justifiably say that
by virtue of his talk, his uses of language, he is "regarded as a sort of real-estate broker." He can indeed
break up "real" estates into imaginary ones. And operative here is a still more suggestive pun. It has to do with
the very good joke about his "seat": "Wherever I sat,
there I might live, and the landscape radiated from me
accordingly. What is a house but a *sedes*, a seat? — better if a country seat." The various meanings of "seat" in
the passage allow us to take "country seat" as a reference
not only to a rural estate. It can also be satiric of that
kind of ownership by referring, in this context, to an old-
fashioned country out-house. The passage brings us,
though less directly than do other parts of the book, to
the subject of excremental vision. Coleridge has given it
a classic definition at the end of his lecture "On Poesy or
Art," and it has had more recent, necessarily more psy-
choanalytic discussion, in Phyllis Greenacre's work on
Swift, in Erik Erickson's magnificent study of young
Luther, and by Norman O. Brown. In *Walden* the subject first emerges from a joke that would be recognized
perhaps only by an ingenious or a dirty mind, were it
not an anticipation of a nearly Shakespearean enhance-
ment of excremental activity that occurs in the penulti-
mate chapter called "Spring" There the excremental
process is equivalent to the formative actions of nature
and the imagination, and man is seen within this process
as "but a mass of thawing clay." Thoreau is at this later

point watching the springtime flow of sand and matter, what he calls "the laboratory of the Artist who made the world and me," and remarks that "This phenomenon is more exhilarating to me than the luxurience and fertility of vineyards. True, it is somewhat excrementitious in its character, and there is no end to the heaps of liver, lights, and bowels, as if the glove itself were turned wrong side outward; but this suggests at least that Nature has some bowels, and there again is mother of humanity." The Swiftean implications of this last phrase are available only when we learn to expect in *Walden* the kind of passionate inventiveness with language that accompanies Thoreau's recognition of the difficulty of his themes.

That Thoreau's process of relinquishment is "excremental" may be taken as his comment on the fact that Emerson divests himself of human form by moving in the opposite direction, upward to the transparency of an eyeball. Both images can be reduced to the same idea of self-surrender and oneness, but it is more important to notice how radically different they are from each other. The contrast is evidence of Thoreau's more insistent effort in style to make the rational, physical, mundane side of a given experience inseparable from its visionary aspects. To put it another way, Thoreau's metaphors are worked out more fully than are Emerson's and in a manner characteristic of the metaphysical poetry they both admired, of Donne's "Good Morrow," for example, or Marvell's "The Garden" in which the speaker absorbs the "all but rude" society, from which he is initially estranged, into a transformed and transforming version of himself. Thoreau is considerably more ambitious for his art than is Emerson, trying stylistically to overcome the split, as Emerson saw it, between the "two lives, of the understanding and the soul." This same ambition for art distinguishes James, Mark Twain, Faulkner, and Fitzgerald in those passages where each tries to cope with the theme of relinquishment and possession.

The point of considering the theme is not that it allows a comparative ranking of writers concerned with it but rather that it helps explain why men of such distinctive individuality can all share a problem of literary expression to a degree that makes it seem indigenous to American literature. My position on the relative genius of these writers is more neutral than I may have suggested. Emerson seems to me a generally much more impressive figure than Thoreau, for example, simply because he *was* more skeptical (and therefore less experimental) about the possible achievements of style in relieving the tensions of "doubleness" or "polarity." He invested less of his energy in stylistic ingenuities than his positions required, but the effect of his relative indifference, compared to Thoreau, is to make him in a curious way more serious than his younger friend about life as ordinarily lived, less the artist-as-show-off, the stylist nearly as fop, and more the reflective adult who sees that, when the writing is all over and the reading is finished, art is still the victim of those aspects of reality that await us outside his pages.

Emerson claims that "nothing is of any value in books excepting the transcendental and extraordinary." This leads him to a position which some modern criticism, with its emphasis on organicism, has deemed heretical — that the most engaging elements of a book are usually those not coherent or organic with the rest. In Emerson's view, writing is valuable for the stimulations offered locally, by particular moments of the reading experience, and not for any retrospective consideration of the whole. With Emerson's criteria it is possible to celebrate the often lamented fact that the classics of American literature are best known for "scenes," passages of writing that cling to the imagination more tenaciously than anything in English fiction, even while, by the same comparison, the books as a whole are almost always flawed by incoherence, by what Yvor Winters calls pseudo-reference, and by excessive ambition.

I do not think it can be argued, for example, that either *The Ambassadors* or *The Bear* succeeds in making moments of visionary possession coherent with the social facts that customarily surround them in fiction or autobiography. It is silly to become moralistic about this situation, as if criticism were obliged to defend some particular forms of reality, to attack Strether, say, for not stepping more boldly into his biological role or for not having wit enough to see what is obviously going on between Chad and Madame de Vionnet. Consideration of the themes of the poet and of relinquishment and possession shows us ways in which our literature can be most interesting when we arrive, through critical evaluation, at the point where we can see in the styles and forms of American classics a struggle to do something impossible.

My own interest is in writers who can be said to be really more *naïvely* ambitious about the consequences of stylistic effort than are Emerson and Cooper. In them, notably for my purposes in Thoreau, Mark Twain, James, and Faulkner, we witness in style and in formal dislocations a kind of drama, all as interesting as the drama involving the characters and usually analogous to it. We can detect a sustained, an acknowledged tension between the writer's commitment to visionary possibilities and his obligations to certain conventions of expression that tend to frustrate those possibilities, to call them into question. This tension, evident in the very syntax of the works we are considering, is a measure of the degree to which visionary experience has to confirm itself within the antagonistic realities of daily life and within the literary artifacts that have shaped those realities. To stress the "tension" or "struggle" in American literature between freedom of consciousness and artificial systems is to raise some doubts about the alleged bareness of American life for novelists in the first half of the nineteenth century. This bareness is supposed by James to have been especially injurious to Hawthorne, but as we move now to consider these two writers in their relationship to one another it might be well to keep in mind Hawthorne's most eloquent complaint, at the opening of *The New Adam and Eve* — that "art" had usurped the place of nature in America:

> We who are born into the world's artificial system can never adequately know how little in our present state and circumstances is natural, and how much is merely the interpolation of the perverted mind and heart of man. Art has become a second and stronger nature; she is a stepmother, whose crafty tenderness has taught us to despise the bountiful and wholesome ministrations of our true parent. It is only through the medium of the imagination that we can lessen those iron fetters, which we call truth and reality, and make ourselves even partially sensible what prisoners we are.

# III

## Visionary to Voyeur:
## Hawthorne and James

James's book on Hawthorne is a study of the American environment from the point of view of the most self-expansive of American writers, and it offers the classic criticism of "the absent things in American life" that a writer presumably needs. Even this early in his career — he had not yet written his more ambitious novels — James reveals the degree to which the self in his work, by which I mean his own projected presence in style, converts and then absorbs other people, other selves, other imaginations. He engrosses his Hawthorne, by a process demonstrable in the style of the book, along with an associated version of "America." This process of self-expansion in James is not preceded by any annihilation of social identity as it is when the American hero tries through the eyes to possess an ideal landscape. Quite the contrary. James's voice in *Hawthorne,* much less in his novels, lays claim to all of Hawthorne's native American virtues enriched by an urbanity that has in it the sounds of London. It was there, at thirty-six, that James wrote the book for the English Men of Letters series.

My procedures here are doubtless open to question: I am selecting very familiar materials, reading them as myths about the Self and about America as an environment for it, and placing this myth within a quasi-historical sequence by which the so-called hero-poet turns his gaze away from the American landscape and becomes an imperialist of the inner lives of other people. As I shall presently show, Hawthorne himself gives us in *The Blithedale Romance* abundant evidence that the process I describe cannot be laid out on a sequential line leading to James. James is only the most evident example of a development; he brings extravagantly to life tendencies which Hawthorne had earlier located, with a sophisticated and critical grasp, in *The Blithedale Romance*.

It would perhaps be more accurate to say that James uses rather than studies Hawthorne. Essentially, the book is James's effort to discover his own relation to New England and to the American past. Geographically, the book embraces Concord, Boston, Cambridge, the area where Hawthorne flourished as a writer and from which James had to absent himself in order to become one. This is the world where his father, long a friend of Emerson, finally settled the James family in 1864, and about which James, a year before the book on Hawthorne, had written the small satiric masterpiece *The Europeans*. Both books are about New England, looked at from a European perspective; and both are about the phenomenon of New England and America before the Civil War. For James, the Civil War marks a divide in the nation, a dividing line between the worlds of his own and of Hawthorne's maturity, a divide in James's own life between a world he associates with

youth and innocence and a European world in which he
has acquired some of the worldliness with which he
speaks of Hawthorne.

When James talks about this division there is an evident discrepancy, noticeable throughout the book on
Hawthorne, between his terms and his tones. The terms
are impersonal and historic; the tone is personally anxious, the self-consciously urbane voice of an American
writing in London who has not yet made a great name
for himself. In stressing the covert elements of the passages that follow — as if they were about James's own
confrontation with various environmental pressures — I
am not saying that the passages or the book have nothing to do with Hawthorne. Nonetheless, we are throughout made as conscious of James's voice as of anything it
has to impart about the earlier American writer. Indeed, the medium which is James's style comes more
strongly across as a subject of the book than does its
announced subject. The reader here encounters characteristics of James different only in degree from what he
will find in the later so-called major phase. A persistent
intrusion of James's personality into the simplest facts,
a consequent swelling and stylization of them is, for example, evident in James's biographical introduction of
Hawthorne:

> Hawthorne sprang from the primitive New
> England stock; he had a very definite and con-
> spicuous pedigree. He was born at Salem, Mas-
> sachusetts, on the 4th of July, 1804, and his
> birthday was the great American festival, the
> anniversary of the Declaration of national In-
> dependence. Hawthorne was in his disposition

an unqualified and unflinching American; he
found occasion to give us the measure of the
fact during the seven years that he spent in
Europe towards the close of his life; and this
was no more than proper on the part of a man
who had enjoyed the honour of coming into
the world on the day on which of all the days
in the year the great Republic enjoys her acut-
est fit of self-consciousness. Moreover, a person
who has been ushered into life by the ringing
of bells and the booming of cannon (unless indeed he be frightened straight out of it again
by the uproar of his awakening) receives by
this very fact an injunction to do something
great, something that will justify such striking
natal accompaniments.

This same stylistic expansiveness, by which simple American materials are made subservient to the speaker's
sophistication, is apparent in the introduction of Hawthorne as a distinctly New England man of letters:

. . . in the field of letters, Hawthorne is the
most valuable example of the American genius. That genius has not, as a whole, been literary; but Hawthorne was on his limited scale a
master of expression. He is the writer to whom
his countrymen most confidently point when
they wish to make a claim to have enriched the
mother-tongue, and, judging from present ap-
pearances, he will long occupy this honourable
position. If there is something very fortunate
for him in the way that he borrows an added
relief from the absence of competitors in his

own line, and from the general flatness of the literary field that surrounds him, there is also, to a spectator, something almost touching in his situation. He was so modest and delicate a genius that we may fancy him appealing from the lonely honour of a representative attitude — perceiving a painful incongruity between his imponderable literary baggage and the large conditions of American life. Hawthorne, on the one side, is so subtle and slender and unpretending, and the American world, on the other, is so vast and various and substantial, that it might seem to the author of *The Scarlet Letter* and the *Mosses from an Old Manse,* that we render him a poor service in contrasting his proportions with those of a great civilisation. But our author must accept the awkward as well as the graceful side of his fame; for he has the advantage of pointing a valuable moral. This moral is that the flower of art blooms only where the soil is deep, that it takes a great deal of history to produce a little literature, that it needs a complex social machinery to set a writer in motion. American civilisation has hitherto had other things to do than to produce flowers, and before giving birth to writers it has wisely occupied itself with providing something for them to write about. Three or four beautiful talents of trans-Atlantic growth are the sum of what the world usually recognises, and in this modest nosegay the genius of Hawthorne is admitted to have the rarest and sweetest fragrance.

His very simplicity has been in his favour; it has helped him to appear complete and homogeneous. To talk of his being national would be to force the note and make a mistake of proportion; but he is, in spite of the absence of the realistic quality, intensely and vividly local. Out of the soil of New England he sprang — in a crevice of that immitigable granite he sprouted and bloomed. Half of the interest that he possesses for an American reader with any turn for analysis must reside in his latent New England savour; and I think it no more than just to say that whatever entertainment he may yield to those who know him at a distance, it is an almost indispensable condition of properly appreciating him to have received a personal impression of the manners, the morals, indeed of the very climate, of the great region of which the remarkable city of Boston is the metropolis. The cold, bright air of New England seems to blow through his pages, and these, in the opinion of many people, are the medium in which it is most agreeable to make the acquaintance of that tonic atmosphere.

The image of nourishment from the American soil occurs as frequently in this book as in *The Europeans,* carrying with it the idea that America is too barren to produce any but the more simple forms of literary life. Modest and delicate, Hawthorne gives off a fragrance necessarily rare, since the American soil can sustain so few blossoms. He is part of a nosegay, of a tiny rustic bouquet. There is something tender in James's image;

there is, equally, something patronizing and superior in his tone. This combination of attitudes is nicely calculated to communicate Hawthorne's function for James: he is an "example," a point of reference by which James defines himself. But his imperialistic inclinations fortunately prevent him from simply contrasting himself to Hawthorne or from contrasting their situations. To do so would be to surrender those American virtues which he attributes to Hawthorne as a representative fellow countryman. Instead, James wants to suggest that these attributes exist in himself in a yet more inclusive form. The complications in his relationship to Hawthorne can be heard in the remark that "American civilization has hitherto had other things to do than to produce flowers, and before giving birth to writers it has wisely occupied itself with providing something for them to write about." The supercilious vagueness of "other things" or of "something" is nonetheless accompanied by an implicit rebuff to the common English assumption that Americans are concerned for prosperity as an end in itself, a rebuff delivered in a tone that shows how far James has himself traveled from this earlier America. While indicating that he is not to be judged as a product of so uncongenial an environment as Hawthorne's, James is nonetheless laying claim to it as a unique heritage. What was to become James's tender-critical relationship to his American heroes and heroines in his novels is very much in evidence here, and the result is equally self-aggrandizing. I evoke the novels as a parallel to the study of Hawthorne in order to insist that I am using a term like self-aggrandizement to describe a quality in James's *writing,* one of the most important sources of its energy. I am not making any

moral judgments about James as an emotional or psychological tycoon.

One aspect of Hawthorne's reputed deprivations is
that America, before that Fall which was the Civil War,
gave him no opportunity to develop a talent for precisely the kind of complex relationships, personal and
cultural, implicit in James's treatment of him, in the
tone, the style by which James defines himself with respect to this "American of an earlier, simpler type." In
James's mythologizing of American history, the Civil
War brought to the American consciousness a sense of
differences, of shades, of complicated relationships:
North and South, rural and urban, agrarian and capital-
istic, cavalier and Yankee, Eden and the Fallen world
— such are the terms used to describe the phenomena.
For that matter, *Hawthorne* allows us to say that the
Civil War also helped create James, the great novelist of
contrast and comparison, and if Hawthorne was a "valu-
able example" of the earlier type of American genius,
James's study of him is in part an announcement that
James is himself an example of a later type:

> . . . the Civil War marks an era in the his-
> tory of the American mind. It introduced into
> the national consciousness a certain sense of
> proportion and relation, of the world being a
> more complicated place than it had hitherto
> seemed, the future more treacherous, success
> more difficult. At the rate at which things are
> going, it is obvious that good Americans will
> be more numerous than ever; but the good
> American, in days to come, will be a more crit-
> ical person than his complacent and confident

grandfather. He has eaten of the tree of knowledge. He will not, I think, be a sceptic, and
still less, of course, a cynic; but he will be,
without discredit to his well-known capacity
for action, an observer. He will remember that
the ways of the Lord are inscrutable, and that
this is a world in which everything happens;
and eventualities, as the late Emperor of the
French used to say, will not find him intellec-
tually unprepared. The good American of
which Hawthorne was so admirable a specimen
was not critical, and it was perhaps for this reason that Franklin Pierce seemed to him a very
proper President.

This is recognizably a description of James, the spectator and the observer, and of those characters, like
Ralph Touchett and Strether, for whom he shows a conspicuous affection.

Making it seem, as he uncharacteristically does in
*Hawthorne,* that literary qualities proceed largely from
social and historical circumstance, James then invents
the qualities in Hawthorne to fit the circumstance: of an
unnourishing American environment. Because he wants
to believe in the bareness of American life before the
war and that, because of it, no serious fiction could have
been written, James seriously diminishes and distorts
Hawthorne's accomplishment. What can he mean, for example, by the central charge that Hawthorne never calls
"things deeply into question"? What are "things" for
Henry James? He cannot mean moral "things" or metaphysical "things" or psychological "things," all of which
he finds abundantly in Hawthorne. By "things" he can

only mean social furniture, manners and appurtenances. It is a deficiency of these "things" in Hawthorne's America that James is famous for evoking in explanation of Hawthorne's failures. The passage is worth quoting, even though it is already too well known, because James's tone modifies his assertions to a degree that has gone unnoticed. He begins by relating "consciousness" to environment in a way obviously relevant to some of the connections I have been trying to make":

> If Hawthorne had been a young Englishman, or a young Frenchman of the same degree of genius, the same cast of mind, the same habits, his consciousness of the world around him would have been a very different affair; however obscure, however reserved, his own personal life, his sense of the life of his fellow-mortals would have been almost infinitely more various. The negative side of the spectacle on which Hawthorne looked out, in his contemplative saunterings and reveries, might, indeed, with a little ingenuity, be made almost ludicrous; one might enumerate the items of high civilisation, as it exists in other countries, which are absent from the texture of American life, until it should become a wonder to know what was left. No State, in the European sense of the word, and indeed barely a specific national name. No sovereign, no court, no personal loyalty, no aristocracy, no church, no clergy, no army, no diplomatic service, no country gentlemen, no palaces, no castles, nor manors, nor old country-houses, nor parson-

ages, nor thatched cottages, nor ivied ruins; no cathedrals, nor abbeys, nor little Norman churches; no great Universities nor public schools — no Oxford, nor Eton, nor Harrow; no literature, no novels, no museums, no pictures, no political society, no sporting class — no Epsom nor Ascot! Some such list as that might be drawn up of the absent things in American life—especially in the American life of forty years ago, the effect of which, upon an English or a French imagination, would probably, as a general thing, be appalling. The natural remark, in the almost lurid light of such an indictment, would be that if these things are left out, everything is left out. The American knows that a good deal remains; what it is that remains — that is his secret, his joke, as one may say. It would be cruel, in this terrible denudation, to deny him the consolation of his natural gift, that "American humour" of which of late years we have heard so much.

The peculiarity in this passage is that it equivocates by exaggeration, by mimicry of a shallow (should one say "English"?) view of what constitutes society: "No Epsom nor Ascot!" The exclamation mark satirizes the extreme reach of the attitudes developed up to that moment in the paragraph. Such equivocation extends also to the nature of his argument about Hawthorne's literary accomplishments. Though we are told at one point that Hawthorne's imagination made him "an *habitué* of a region of mysteries and subtleties," we are told at another that it was "cold and light and thin."

The metaphor of "thinness" reminds us that "thickness" and reality for James in this book consist of social life, not the life of "shadows." Hawthorne's society, it is observed at still another point, was "simple, democratic, thinly composed" so that for a writer who was in any case "little disposed to multiply his relations" America offered no "variety or intimacy of relations" — James's appetite and capacity for which is of the very essence of his marvelously supple tones of voice.

James can of course be right about symptoms and wrong in his diagnosis. There is no denying, as Lionel Trilling shows, some of James's characterizations of Hawthorne, and we are informed by these of essential differences between the two writers and between the worlds to which each belonged. Thematically, for example, "The Maypole of Merrymount" and *The Europeans* are much alike. Each is about a contest between what Hawthorne calls "jollity and gloom" for dominion in New England; each is enacted in a New England dominated either by Puritanism or, in James's novel, by some later modified form of it. But the *way* in which the contending forces are defined and in which the narrator sounds in each work is radically different. The characters and James himself as narrator of *The Europeans* are wholly defined by their tones of voice, by their conduct in dialogue and in social relations, and by the extent to which they can deal with the phenomenon of the Baroness Eugenia, confronting her American relatives with her "large element of costume." Everyone in the novel is revealed through verbal, social, and sexual manners, and the differentiations are extremely delicate and exacting. By contrast, nothing can be inferred from the way the characters sound

in Hawthorne's story; they have no existence in the social and sexual world where James's characters come
to life. As a narrator, Hawthorne in this instance projects no social class or type; he never observes social
conduct, but only the degree to which his characters
are submissive to allegorical definition. James is accurate enough when he complains that Hawthorne "had
certainly not proposed to himself to give an account
of the social idiosyncrasies of his fellow citizens."

But if James is able to locate symptoms of social
deprivation in Hawthorne, he is not very successful in
his diagnosis of them. An essential qualification to his
argument is that even if Hawthorne's world was as socially thin as he claimed it was, Hawthorne's qualities as
a writer are not significantly explained by this fact. It
seems never to occur to James that Hawthorne's accuracy of observation actually depends on that "shad-
owy style of portraiture" which he takes to be a fault. In
James's account Hawthorne practically has no environment as a fund of novelistic suggestion, a peculiar
lamentation from a novelist who in his own works often
tries to free his characters from environmental pressures. Hawthorne can thus be "redolent of the social system in which he had his being" and still have "none of
the apparatus of an historian," because presumably
America has produced nothing that excites a novelist
into being a historian of manners. Again, Hawthorne is
"thin" because America is "thin." In *The Europeans*
James, the year before, wrote a novel about Hawthorne's own time and place which Hawthorne himself presumably could not have written. He literally
brings into that "thin" environment an element of
contrast — the Europeans — without which the sweet

but essentially silent American could have no novelistic existence.

Missing from James's account is the ample evidence from Hawthorne's fiction and especially from his prefaces that, far from feeling deprived by what James thinks is lacking in his society, Hawthorne was usually anxious to escape from what it did offer. Nearly every novel and story is about his own and his characters' entrapment in what he called "artificial system," the controls exerted over consciousness not only by social organizations but by literary conventions. James has his reasons for insisting that Hawthorne was victimized by the social "thinness" of his environment; but any reader, without James's motives, is able to see that Hawthorne was much more the victim of literary "thickness," of "art" or "artificial system."

Even leaving allegory aside for the moment, there are few writers who tell us so often that his stories are derived from sources other than life, and no writer who so often tells us that his own characters have already fashioned their experience according to literary conventions. In many of his stories and longer works Hawthorne plays the avowed role of an investigator into materials he has inherited both in detail and in the shape that historians or other writers have given them. His allegories are themselves presented less as his invention than as hearsay, as anecdotes, as an artificial formation imposed on life of some earlier time. Romantic, melodramatic, and supernatural events come from his pages in the form of old wives' tales and gossip, products of the popular imagination toward which Hawthorne strikes the pose, as so often in *The House of the Seven Gables,* of a worldly and amused skeptic:

We have already hinted that it is not our purpose to trace down the history of the Pyncheon family, in its unbroken connection with the House of the Seven Gables; nor to show, as in a magic picture, how the rustiness and infirmity of age gathered over the venerable house itself. As regards its interior life, a large, dim looking-glass used to hang in one of the rooms, and was fabled to contain within its depths all the shapes that had ever been reflected there, — the old Colonel himself, and his many descendants, some in the garb of antique babyhood, and others in the bloom of feminine beauty or manly prime, or saddened with the wrinkles of frosty age. Had we the secret of that mirror, we would gladly sit down before it, and transfer its revelations to our page. But there was a story, for which it is difficult to conceive any foundation, that the posterity of Matthew Maule had some connection with the mystery of the looking-glass, and that, by what appears to have been a sort of mesmeric process, they could make its inner region all alive with the departed Pyncheons; not as they had shown themselves to the world nor in their better and happier hours, but as doing over again some deed of sin, or in the crisis of life's bitterest sorrow. The popular imagination, indeed, long kept itself busy with the affair of the old Puritan Pyncheon and the wizard Maule; the curse, which the latter flung from his scaffold, was remembered, with the very important addition, that it had become a part of the Pyncheon inheritance. If one of the family did but gurgle in his throat, a bystander would be likely enough to whisper, between jest and earnest, "He has Maule's blood to drink!" The sudden death of a Pyncheon, about a hundred years ago, with circumstances very similar to what have been related of the Colonel's exit, was held as giving additional probability to the received opinion on this topic. It was considered, moreover, an ugly and ominous circumstance, that Colonel Pyncheon's picture — in obedience, it was said, to a provision of his will — remain affixed to the wall of the room in which he died. Those stern, immitigable features seemed to symbolize an evil influence, and so darkly to mingle the shadow of their presence with the sunshine of the passing hour, that no good thoughts or purposes could ever spring up and blossom there. To the thoughtful mind there will be no tinge of superstition in what we figuratively express, by affirming that the ghost of a dead progenitor — perhaps as a portion of his own punishment — is often doomed to become the Evil Genius of his family.

The narrator simultaneously offers and discredits his material: nearly the entire substance of the paragraph is accredited to fable, superstition, or "story" for which "it is difficult to conceive any foundation." But the accumulated effect of "fable," full of inventiveness and empowered by popular belief, is allowed to take altogether firmer hold on our imagination than the narrator's

skepticism, which is repetitive and tiresome. The reader
is at least half the time bored if not impatient. Indeed in
his novels Hawthorne locally is often less than enliven-
ing; he is the sort of writer more impressive in retro-
spect, in some memory of a scene rather than in the
reading of it. In the paragraph just quoted, the power
evoked in, say, reports of popular superstition is continually dulled by narrative play or caution or tasteless literariness. He has an irritating reluctance to put his
"toys" away, even after they have created situations that
cry out for a finish that is dramatically simple. One
regrettable instance is the death in *The Blithedale Romance* of Zenobia. The effectively brutal description of
dragging the river for her body is glossed with the
hideously "literary" sentence, "Black River of Death,
thou hast yielded up thy victim! Zenobia was found."
The remark is not placed in such a way as to constitute a
revelation of narrator Coverdale's persistently "literary"
responses to events, so that it scarcely matters that such a
sentence is an echo of Gothic fiction. And in any case,
Hawthorne's literariness is just as often without any distinguished literary antecedent or even a possible function. Nearly all of *The Marble Faun* is written in the
unfortunate style of feminine travel guides and bro-
chures:

> These foreign guests are indeed ungrateful, if
> they do not breathe a prayer for Pope Clem-
> ent, or whatever Holy Father it may have
> been, who levelled the summit of the mount so
> skilfully, and bounded it with the parapet of
> the city wall; who laid out those broad walks
> and drives, and overhung them with the deep-

ening shade of many kinds of tree; who scattered the flowers of all seasons, and of every clime, abundantly over those green, central lawns; who scooped out hollows, in fit places, and, setting great basins of marble in them, caused ever-gushing fountains to fill them to the brim; who reared up the immemorial obelisk out of the soil that had long hidden it; who placed pedestals along the borders of the avenues, and crowned them with busts of that multitude of worthies — statesmen, heroes, artists, men of letters and of song — whom the whole world claims as its chief ornaments, though Italy produced them all. In a word, the Pincian garden is one of the things that reconcile the stranger (since he fully appreciates the enjoyment, and feels nothing of the cost) to the rule of an irresponsible dynasty of Holy Fathers, who seem to have aimed at making life as agreeable an affair as it can well be.

Hawthorne's characters often exist in their relations to one another much as Hawthorne exists here in his relation to the reader. Their speech gives them less the reality of created life than a role that reminds us of how preposterously they belong to "art." " 'Pooh, pooh, master high-sheriff,' cried the lieutenant-governor" — this line at the beginning of *The House of the Seven Gables* and before the discovery of Colonel Pyncheon's body is fortunately an extreme but unfortunately not an unusual instance.

And yet, the barrier of "art" between human beings, the barrier created by role-taking, is something that in

Hawthorne's best work exists not as a defect or a pretention but as his veritable subject matter, as *the* problem both for himself and for his characters in relation to the people they are addressing. Thus, Chapter XVII of *The Scarlet Letter,* the chapter in which Hester and Dimmesdale come closest to opening their hearts to one another, is entitled "The Pastor and His Parishoner," as if to suggest that they cannot meet without the defenses between them of some kind of officialese, of roles that prevent their directly confronting one another. Similarly, "The Maypole of Merrymount" is populated by representatives of the two forces contending for empire in the new world, and it is significant that the forces are defined primarily in literary rather than in moral terms: allegory (the Puritans) defeats pastoral (the revelers). It is as if Hawthorne were saying, as indeed he does say even more directly in other stories and in his prefaces, that the control exerted on the imagination by literary conventions is indistinguishable from the theological or political conventions found here and in *The Scarlet Letter*. Hawthorne's employment of what James calls the "poetic and aesthetic point of view" is full of moral and human urgency. For him a judgment from this point of view reveals the degree to which any given form of "art" has suppressed or perverted human nature.

There is in Hawthorne some of the Swedenborgianism so eloquently expressed in the writings of the elder James. Hawthorne did not have the personal power, he was not enough of an identified or identifiable person, as the fluctuations of his narrative voice sufficiently indicate, to write with the eloquent, radical distaste for system to be heard in the elder James. And yet his work might be taken as an effort finally to reach the position clarified in the elder James's *Christianity and the Logic of Creation:*

> . . . the life of God in nature . . . is a life of perfect freedom or spontaneity. In that life self-love freely subordinates itself to neighborly love, or promotes its own ends by promoting the welfare of all mankind. But so long as this life is wholly unsuspected by men; so long as no man dreams of any other social destiny for the race than that which it has already realized, and which leaves one man out of all fellowship or equality with another, — self-love is completely unprovided for, except in subtle and hypocritical forms, and is consequently driven to these disorderly assertions of itself by way of actually keeping alive. . . . The liar, the thief, the adulterer, the murderer, no doubt utterly perverts the divine life which is latent in every human form, . . . but he nevertheless does all this in a way of a mute, unconscious protest against an overwhelming social tyranny, which would otherwise crush out the distinctive life of man under the machinery of government and caste. Accordingly I am profoundly convinced that if we had not had some persons of that audacious make which would qualify them to throw off their existing social subjection, and so ventilate, even by infernal airs, the underlying life and freedom of humanity, — that life and freedom would have been utterly stifled. . . . These men have

been, unknown to themselves, the forlorn hope of humanity, plunging headlong into the unfathomable night only that we by the bridge of their desecrated forms might eventually pass over its hideous abyss into the realms of endless day.

The passage might remind us of Hawthorne's confidence that "the medium of imagination" can also "ventilate, even by infernal airs, the underlying life and freedom of humanity." It can, to allude once more to the opening of "The New Adam and Eve," "lessen those iron fetters, which we call truth and reality, and make [us] even partially sensible what prisoners we are." The younger James is obviously unresponsive to this aspect of Hawthorne when he remarks that "in his metaphysical moods, he is nothing if not allegorical and allegory, to my sense, is quite one of the lighter exercises of the imagination." Hawthorne in his metaphysical moods is often not allegorical at all. He is more apt to be trying to suspend us, as in the exquisite and seldom noticed story "The Wives of the Dead," between actuality and dream. Hawthorne investigates the allegorizing tendencies at work in the consciousness of his characters (and in his own), and shows how life is hatefully confined by allegorical rigidities.

The great achievement of "My Kinsman, Major Molineux," as an instance, is that the narrator is full of shock and remorse at the brutality caused by the town's allegorical treatment of Robin's kinsman. Narrator-Hawthorne is of course also himself the Major's kinsman, though this is left entirely to implications of tone and of the historical evocations in the opening

paragraphs. He is a kinsman very different from young
Robin. This "shrewd" boy is an American of a type
earlier than Hawthorne, a pre-Revolutionary American, full of pathetic aspirations to sound like an Englishman, lost and bewildered in his colonial surroundings. Still, he is a keenly instinctive opportunist whose
ultimate "shrewdness," a frequent word in the story,
consists in expelling that part of himself which is England, represented by his kinsman, the Major. Scarcely knowing what has been happening to him, the boy
joins at the end in the horrible community of laughter
— from which the narrator dissociates himself — which
signals the casting out of the tarred and feathered
"potentate." For the narrator, however, they are not
throwing out "England"; they are instead "trampling
all on an old man's heart," a phrase meant to dissuade
the reader from being as crudely allegorical as the town.
Even as it emerges, the American community is thus
characterized as inhumane and categorical in its handling of human beings, though these are made to seem
necessary faults in a world wherein the workings of reality, of history, even of dreams are also victimized by "artificial system." It is hinted not that the story *is* a dream
— "Well, Robin, are you dreaming?" the boy is asked by
a townsman at the end — but that it easily might be
one: this social-climbing boy, frustrated in his search
through the town for that element of "authority" who
is his English kinsman, becomes, through exhaustion,
ready to wish the Major out of his blood, out of his
speech, out of that community of raucous Americans
among whom at the end he is promised that "you may
rise in the world without the help of your kinsman,
Major Molineux."

At its most interesting, Hawthorne's fiction is in the American literary tradition of stylistic struggle. In his case, the struggle is not only to reveal the limitations of Puritan allegory; it is also to cast off the restraints of literary and social artificiality. He did not often succeed, as he brilliantly does in "My Kinsman, Major Molineux," and D. H. Lawrence is surely right in his exasperation with *The Scarlet Letter* for its submission to moral standards against which the book is always gathering its force. From my point of view, his greatest achievement is *The Blithedale Romance,* and it also happens to be a novel that clarifies the degree to which James was unable to see either the genius of Hawthorne or the extent to which Hawthorne's concern for the self and its environment resembled what were to be his own later preoccupations. To a surprising degree, Coverdale is an anticipation of the hero of *The Ambassadors,* though James could hardly have known this when he wrote his study of Hawthorne in 1879.

## II

The achievement for Hawthorne of *The Blithedale Romance* is that he cast his own preciosities, his own evasiveness and finickiness into a character. And yet he treats this character with an extraordinary degree of critical compassion. He makes of Coverdale a masterly historical, as well as a personal and artistic creation. It is tempting to think of Hawthorne's accomplishment as one almost of historical prediction. Coverdale is an example of the particular kind of sensibility that was to find fuller expression in those crucial years 1890–1914 when modern literature had its birth.

In one sense *The Blithedale Romance* is about the re-
forming zeal of the early part of the nineteenth century
becoming, in talented individuals, a personal withdrawal into good taste and "sensibility." The connection
between reform of and retreat from society is, of course,
implicit in everything that Emerson writes about the
transcendentalist as a type, and as I have argued in
*The Comic Sense of Henry James,* that type, as defined by Emerson, is close to the unradical figure Osmond of *The Portrait of a Lady.* For both Emerson
and Hawthorne monomania was the occupational dis-
ease of reformers like Hollingsworth, but they also
recognized, as A. N. Kaul has noticed in *The American
Vision,* that one consequence of idealism gone sour can
be the self-absorbed fastidiousness of a character like
Coverdale — or Osmond. Coverdale's mockery of his
own participation in the Blithedale community involves
his conscious confusion of Emersonian images with conflicting images and tones of social dandyism. The characterization of Coverdale by means of his highly allusive
speech reveals once again Hawthorne's extraordinary
sensitivity to the way in which human conduct is an
imitation of old rather than a source of new literary
images or tropes.

One quite startling example is the opening of Chapter XII, "Coverdale's Hermitage":

> Long since, in this part of our circumjacent
> wood, I had found out for myself a little her-
> mitage. It was a kind of leafy cave, high up-
> ward into the air, among the midmost
> branches of a white-pine tree. A grape-vine,
> of unusual size and luxuriance, had twined

and twisted itself up into the tree, and, after wreathing the entanglement of its tendrils around almost every bough, had caught hold of three or four neighboring trees, and married the whole clump with a perfectly inextricable knot of polygamy. Once, while sheltering myself from a summer shower, the fancy had taken me to clamber up into this seemingly impervious mass of foliage. The branches yielded me a passage, and closed again, beneath, as if only a squirrel or a bird had passed. Far aloft, around the stem of the central pine, behold, a perfect nest for Robinson Crusoe or King Charles! A hollow chamber, of rare seclusion, had been formed by the decay of some of the pine branches, which the vine had lovingly strangled with its embrace, burying them from the light of day in an aerial sepulchre of its own leaves. It cost me but little ingenuity to enlarge the interior, and open loopholes through the verdant walls. Had it ever been my fortune to spend a honey-moon, I should have thought seriously of inviting my bride up thither, where our next neighbors would have been two orioles in another part of the clump.

It was an admirable place to make verses, tuning the rhythm to the breezy symphony that so often stirred among the vine-leaves; or to meditate an essay for the Dial, in which the many tongues of Nature whispered mysteries, and seemed to ask only a little stronger puff of wind, to speak out the solution of its riddle. Being so pervious to air-currents, it was just the

nook, too, for the enjoyment of a cigar. This
hermitage was my one exclusive possession,
while I counted myself a brother of the social-
ists. It symbolized my individuality, and aided
me in keeping it inviolate. None ever found
me out in it, except, once, a squirrel. I brought
thither no guest, because, after Hollingsworth
failed me, there was no longer the man alive
with whom I could think of sharing all. So
there I used to sit, owl-like, yet not without
liberal and hospitable thoughts. I counted the
innumerable clusters of my vine, and fore-
reckoned the abundance of my vintage. It
gladdened me to anticipate the surprise of the
Community, when, like an allegorical figure of
rich October, I should make my appearance,
with shoulders bent beneath the burthen of
ripe grapes, and some of the crushed ones
crimsoning my brow as with a blood-stain.

Ascending into this natural turret, I peeped,
in turn, out of several of its small windows.
The pine-tree, being ancient, rose high above
the rest of the wood, which was of compara-
tively recent growth. Even where I sat, about
midway between the root and the topmost
bough, my position was lofty enough to serve
as an observatory, not for starry investigations,
but for those sublunary matters in which lay a
lore as infinite as that of the planets. Through
one loop-hole, I saw the river lapsing calmly
onward, while, in the meadow near its brink,
a few of the brethren were digging peat for our
winter's fuel. On the interior cart-road of our

> farm, I discerned Hollingsworth, with a yoke
> of oxen hitched to a drag of stones, that were
> to be piled into a fence, on which we employed
> ourselves at the odd intervals of other labor.
> The harsh tones of his voice, shouting to the
> sluggish steers, made me sensible, even at such
> a distance, that he was ill at ease, and that the
> baulked philanthropist had the battle-spirit in
> his heart.

Coverdale's physical situation is made typical of a recurrent one in American literature precisely that we may see it as a significant variation. The account of his retreat from society into an "ideal" community and from there into sequestered landscape has affinities with those scenes in American literature of which the opening of Emerson's *Nature* is a paradigm. He is in a position here to take an elevated view of landscape, or of natural phenomenon, a position comparable to Cooper's Deerslayer, Melville's Foretopman, Henry James's Milly Theale, first seen in *The Wings of the Dove* sitting on the edge of a cliff, "in a state of uplifted and unlimited possession that had nothing to gain from violence." The recurrent posture has already been described. And in the way he sounds, Coverdale here asks to be compared with Thoreau: "So there I used to sit, owl-like, yet not without liberal and hospitable thoughts. I counted the innumerable clusters of my vine, and fore-reckoned the abundance of my vintage."

Yet, these analogies between Coverdale and the favored types of American romantic literature are all as quickly distorted by his peculiarity as is the analogy between him and the Emersonian type to which he bears

superficial resemblances. Thus having sounded like
Thoreau, he immediately slips into an easy literary
allegorization of himself, the planning of a "literary"
role, that Thoreau would have found contemptible: "It
gladdened me to anticipate the surprise of the Community, when, like an allegorical figure of rich October, I
should make my appearance, with shoulders bent beneath the burthen of ripe grapes, and some of the
crushed ones crimsoning my brow as with a blood
stain." The rendering of his Emersonian affinities is in a
tone no less satiric and dandified: he would "meditate an
essay for 'The Dial,' in which the many tongues of Nature whispered mysteries, and seemed to ask only a little
stronger puff of wind to speak out the solution of its riddle. Being so pervious to air-currents, it was just the
nook, too, for the enjoyment of a cigar." A somewhat
sickly, somewhat even masturbatory quality in Coverdale's self-regarding retreat is evident even in the images
describing it. It is as if he were retreating into a state
not of heightened consciousness but of death. He is
dead in the sense that he shows no capacity for union
with others or within nature as he adduces it. It will be
noticed that his hiding place results from what he calls
the "inextricable knot of polygamy" among the bows of
the trees and the grape vine. But the image of "polygamy" and of marriage are in Coverdale's mind connected with death: the vine had "lovingly strangled
with its embrace" some of the pine branches; and the
bride whom he would bring to his hide-out ought to be
warned that he thinks of it as "an aerial sepulchre."
More revealing than these images, however, is the self-
titillating ghoulishness of Coverdale's tone. His "worldliness" gets expressed in a childlike, provocative contempt for the ordinary human customs of society.

If, as I think, Hawthorne is here showing us the transformations of a sort of Emersonian man into a Dandy,
then he should be credited too with seeing in the dandy
much that Baudelaire was to see in him. Baudelaire's
dandy also allows us to take his evident superiority of
feeling as a form of stoicism and spirituality, and as
Roger Shattuck says, this sophisticated man of many
masks insists on wearing his childhood as the charm over
his heart. But what is given as a positive portrait of the
Dandy-Child in Baudelaire is in Hawthorne hedged
with qualifications directed not only toward the personal morality of Coverdale but also toward those features he incorporates, in the corrupt form of Dandy and
Child, out of Emerson.

Hawthorne shows here an unusually self-confident
treatment of human postures customarily exempted in
classic American literature from psychological penetration. Figures communing with nature abound in that
literature but they are essentially the same whether they
seek purification from nature or try to impose their
wills upon it. In either case they are enacting the same
conviction, so pronounced in Coverdale, that participation in society can only thwart the exercise of feelings
that are most God-like. This supposition in Hawthorne's
Coverdale is made the rationale for a kind of non-sexual
voyeurism. In his lofty obsevatory he is not interested in
"starry investigations," as is Huck Finn at his bedroom
window. Rather he watches "those sublunary matters in
which lay a lore as infinite as that of the planets." Even
when he expresses some interest in natural surroundings
it is in an analogy that reveals much greater excitement
about being a peeping Tom: "I abated my pace, and
looked about me into the innermost sanctuary of this
green cathedral, just as, in human acquaintance, a

casual opening sometimes lets us, all of a sudden, into the long-sought intimacy of a mysterious heart." These attitudes are not intrinsically voyeuristic or unappealing. But they are made so by Coverdale's style — the extravagance of his metaphors when responding to ordinary human gestures, his insistent evocations of the covert, his "approved" rhetoric about "long-sought intimacy," all come from a man incapable of human fellowship.

Not surprisingly Coverdale can as easily carry on his activities of retreat and observation in town as in the country. Again, Hawthorne reveals a genius for cultural criticism of a kind indistinguishable from psychological portraiture when he endows Coverdale's language with images familiar to any reader of romantic literature:

> Bewitching to my fancy are all those nooks and crannies, where Nature, like a stray partridge, hides her head among the long-established haunts of men! It is likewise to be remarked, as a general rule, that there is far more of the picturesque, more truth to native and characteristic tendencies, and vastly greater suggestiveness, in the back view of a residence, whether in town or country, than in its front. The latter is always artificial; it is meant for the world's eye, and is therefore a veil and a concealment.

Such accents can be heard in Cooper or in Emerson: the taste for the picturesque (so strong also in early James), the contempt for the "world's eye" that can see only what is "artificial," the pride in seeing beyond the "veil" and "concealment," which is the front of things, and into a more essential reality.

What Coverdale sees out of his window in town is a
still more foppish version of those conventions that he
himself perverts. Looking across the way, he observes
the preparations of a sartorial dandy:

> In one of the upper chambers, I saw a young
> man in a dressing-gown, standing before the
> glass and brushing his hair, for a quarter-of-an-
> hour together. He then spent an equal space of
> time in the elaborate arrangement of his cra-
> vat, and finally made his appearance in a dress-
> coat, which I suspected to be newly come from
> the tailor's, and now first put on for a dinner-
> party.

Coverdale might be thought of as Hawthorne's reply for
such patronization as he was to receive from James. He
is a parody of a figure common in James's fiction — of
the man who finds in Style, in the "picturesque," in observing manners and customs, in extorting secrets from
social interchange, the kind of exhilaration that earlier
American heroes found in a communion with natural
surroundings or in the violent activity that could take
place between the hero and elements of his natural environment.

It is Hawthorne's genius in *The Blithedale Romance*
to have given novelistic reality to a complicated development in human consciousness. He shows how the romantic dream of creating an environment for the self
rather than submitting to the environment authorized
by "artificial systems" becomes a form of aestheticism.
Coverdale thus admires his little nook because its pro-
tection from the "many tongues of Nature" allows him
"the enjoyment of a cigar." Despite the vulgarity of his
ambitions, Coverdale is a prediction of the kind of hero,

justifying himself by appeals to superior sensibility, who
occupies the center of such contemporary classics as
those of Joyce, Lawrence, Faulkner, and of course
James. The many distinctions that have to be made
among these writers do not substantially modify a remarkable similarity among them: in each the expressed
contempt for the way the world organizes itself is accompanied by aggressive efforts in the hero's imagination to give it an alternative order. Such efforts, often
defined by American writers in metaphors of artistic
creation, are what Hawthorne prescribes for the imagination and to which he dedicated his own. Thus,
by his own insistence, Coverdale is a "poet." He is also
an anticipation of that later, altogether more lovable
creator, Strether of *The Ambassadors*.

## III

*The Ambassadors* offers remarkably beautiful instances
of the hero's effort to transform the things he sees into
visions, to detach them from time and from the demands of nature, and to give them the composition of
*objets d'art*. The novel is about the cost and profit for
such acts of imagination, and indeed one can feel that
the novel itself pays a price for them. At moments the
demands made by the style on the reader are demonstrably excessive. Precisely at such times James is working
hardest to make Strether's visions-of-reality-as-art into
something like reality for the reader. To do this he
forces us into a kind of suspended time, taking something that is directly impinging upon Strether's consciousness and presenting it, through manipulation of
verb tenses, as something refashioned in Strether's sub-

sequent recollection. Thus, "he was to remember again
repeatedly the medal-like Italian face, in which every
line was an artist's own." Such manipulation is very
much like that carried out by Coverdale in, for instance,
his being "gladdened . . . to anticipate the surprise of
the Community, when, like an allegorical figure of rich
October, I should make my appearance." That the
whole of *The Blithedale Romance* is narrated in retro-
spect gives to Coverdale's narrative about his experience
all the attributes of a novelistic one or, since he calls
himself a poet, of someone who fashions or shapes events
as if they belonged not in real time but in the patterned
time of art. And like Strether he must face the anguish
of finding that life, notably the lives of others, will not
be shaped by the often conflicting pressures of his aestheticism and his morality:

> Of all possible observers, me thought, a
> woman, like Zenobia, and a man like Hollings-
> worth, should have selected me. And, now,
> when the event has long been past, I retain the
> same opinion of my fitness for the office. True;
> I might have condemned them. Had I been
> judge, as well as witness, my sentence might
> have been stern as that of Destiny itself. But,
> still, no trait of original nobility of character;
> no struggle against temptation, — no iron ne-
> cessity of will, on the one hand, nor extenuat-
> ing circumstance to be derived from passion
> and despair, on the other, — no remorse that
> might coëxist with error, even if powerless to
> prevent it, — no proud repentance that should
> claim retribution as a meed — would go un-

appreciated. True, again, I might give my
full assent to the punishment which was sure
to follow. But it would be given mournfully,
and with undiminished love. And, after all was
finished, I would come, as if to gather up the
white ashes of those who had perished at the
stake, and to tell the world — the wrong being
now atoned for — how much had perished
there, which it had never yet known how to
praise.

The passage is Jamesian in a number of ways, notably in
the character's pretension that he is the guardian of
other people's experience. Coverdale imagines his lovers
in a melodrama wherein they enact more than the
world, but not more than he, can see and appreciate. If
one leaves the melodrama aside, along with the offensive
character it exhibits, the roles in the passage might be
occupied by Strether, Chad, and Madame de Vionnet.
These last two also fail, of course, to live up to the
imagination of the man observing them.

I have already suggested how in Coverdale Hawthorne has managed to objectify certain tendencies in
himself that are essentially childish and trivializing,
how, as Frederick Crews puts it in *The Sins of the Fathers*, the novel is "a self-critical comedy." In Coverdale
Hawthorne scutinizes his own tendency to soften reality
by giving it the quality of art — as if what happens were,
say, a pastoral or melodrama — and of then equivocating
in his relation to the reader by becoming a teasing inter-
locuter between him and the elusiveness of reality thus
transformed. Hawthorne is at his best when he becomes
the critic of what otherwise victimizes him: the distor-

tions of reality by art or by style. And at his best, as in
*The Blithedale Romance,* he is closest to James. Early
and late — in *The Europeans,* in *The Spoils of Poynton,*
in *The Ambassadors* and *The Golden Bowl* — James is
fascinated by theatrical behavior or by situations in
which people are treated as *objets d'art*. It is significant
that in these instances there is, as in the Hawthorne of
*Blithedale,* a marked degree of personal projection into
the central characters and with it a degree of self-criti-
cism. At the simplest level there is Eugenia in *The Europeans,* whose large "element of costume," both verbal
and household, is as little understood around Boston as
were some of James's own indulgences in elaborateness
of style; at a later more complicated stage there is an
aspect of James enacted both by Fleda Vetch and by
Strether when they see reality in images that remove it
from time and nature. Leo Bersani, in his extraordinary essay on *The Wings of the Dove,** shows how
James's omnivorousness about possible significances results in his use of the mind of Densher to conjure up
images and posibilities that really cannot at all belong
to Densher's own experience of what is happening.
These images remain in the book as evidences of how
James, not Densher, is working off, as it were, an excess
of psychological and social inventiveness. In James, as in
Hawthorne's creation of Coverdale, there is both a criticism of characters who perhaps care too much about
merely "seeing into" things, even while there is a fascination, sometimes close to delight, in the moments thus
produced. Having, by the very nature of the imaginations that engendered them, only a tangential relation to
what is really going on, these moments needn't be *made*

* *Modern Fiction Studies,* VI (Summer, 1960), 131–44.

into anything else, needn't be organic, as the phrase goes, with anything but the creative vision itself. They are, as it were, pure art in being freed from the pressure of any environment but that of the mind from which they issue.

One of the compelling instances in James is the famous scene in Gloriani's garden in *The Ambassadors:*

> This assault of images became for a moment, in the address of the distinguished sculptor, almost formidable: Gloriani showed him, in such perfect confidence, on Chad's introduction of him, a fine worn handsome face, a face that was like an open letter in a foreign tongue. With his genius in his eyes, his manners on his lips, his long career behind him and his honours and rewards all round, the great artist, in the course of a single sustained look and a few words of delight at receiving him, affected our friend as a dazzling prodigy of type. Strether had seen in museums — in the Luxembourg as well as, more reverently, later on, in the New York of the billionaires — the work of his hand; knowing too that after an earlier time in his native Rome he had migrated, in mid-career, to Paris, where, with a personal lustre almost violent, he shone in a constellation: all of which was more than enough to crown him, for his guest, with the light, with the romance, of glory. Strether, in contact with that element as he had never yet so intimately been, had the consciousness of opening to it, for the happy instant, all the

windows of his mind, of letting this rather grey
interior drink in for once the sun of a clime
not marked in his old geography. He was to remember again repeatedly the medal-like Italian face, in which every line was an artist's
own, in which time told only as tone and consecration; and he was to recall in especial, as
the penetrating radiance, as the communication of the illustrious spirit itself, the manner
in which, while they stood briefly, in welcome
and response, face to face, he was held by the
sculptor's eyes. He wasn't soon to forget them,
was to think of them, all unconscious, unin-
tending, preoccupied though they were, as the
source of the deepest intellectual sounding to
which he had ever been exposed. He was in
fact quite to cherish his vision of it, to play
with it in idle hours; only speaking of it to no
one and quite aware he couldn't have spoken
without appearing to talk nonsense. Was what
it had told him or what it had asked him the
greater of the mysteries? Was it the most special flare, unequalled, supreme, of the aesthetic
torch, lighting that wondrous world for ever,
or was it above all the long straight shaft sunk
by a personal acuteness that life had seasoned
to steel? Nothing on earth could have been
stranger and no one doubtless more surprised
than the artist himself, but it was for all the
world to Strether just then as if in the matter of
his accepted duty he had positively been on
trial. The deep human expertness in Gloriani's
charming smile — oh the terrible life behind

it! — was flashed upon him as a test of his
stuff.

Nowhere does the passage ask us to take Strether's
vision as anything but peculiar, as literally un-natural.
It is admitted, for example, that there is no way for him
to turn his vision into ordinary conversation without
"appearing to talk nonsense." The "nonsense" would
consist of the fact that, as Strether sees him, Gloriani is
not a person but a work of art. And yet, James's candor
here is not meant as a criticism of Strether. In Strether,
the tendency to view people and events as art enhances
rather than impoverishes them, unlike the similar tendency exercised by Fleda Vetch and Mrs. Gareth in *The
Spoils of Poynton*. Gloriani is a "dazzling prodigy of
type," his face is like an "open letter," he "shone like a
constellation," the lines in his face being, like those in a
statue or a coin, a "tone and consecration." That these
lines are called "an artist's own," only makes explicit
the metaphor suggested early in the passage in the
reference to "the museums." Far from believing that
Strether would talk such "nonsense," the reader will
perhaps notice that here he is not talking even to us. He
is not, as a matter of fact, even reacting to the scene in
front of him. Instead, we are told how he *was* to react to
it in the future: "he was to remember again repeatedly
the medal-like Italian face" or "he wasn't soon to forget
them, was to think of them, all unconscious, unintend-
ing. . . ."

*The Ambassadors* is essentially about the process enacted in Gloriani's garden, the process of "conversion":
the failed "conversion" of Chad by Madame de Vionnet,
the "conversion" of Strether by Paris into a man whose
capacities for appreciation create a world — alternative

both to Paris and to Woollett and more compelling in
the duties it demands from him than either place could
be. Understandably, the word "conversion," in a con-
tinuation of the scene at which we're looking, takes on
significances that are a mixture of the artistic and the
religious, of pleasure that is also an exaction of a duty.
The masterful placing of the word in the conversation
that follows shows how much James felt at every point
the developing fusion, in the consciousness of his hero
and in this book, of aesthetic and moral feelings. Miss
Barrace initiates the dialogue with the remark:

> "Oh you, Mr. Bilham," she replied as with
> an impatient rap on the glass, "you're not
> worth sixpence! You come over to convert the
> savages — for I know you verily did, I remem-
> ber you — and the savages simply convert
> *you*."
>
> "Not even!" the young man woefully con-
> fessed: "they haven't gone through that form.
> They've simply — the cannibals! — eaten me;
> converted me if you like, but converted me
> into food. I'm but the bleached bones of a
> Christian."
>
> "Well then there we are! Only" — and Miss
> Barrace appealed again to Strether — "don't let
> it discourage you. You'll break down soon
> enough, but you'll meanwhile have had your
> moments. *Il faut en avoir.* I always like to see
> you while you last. And I'll tell you who *will*
> last."
>
> "Waymarsh?" — he had already taken her
> up.
>
> She laughed out as at the alarm of it. "He'll

resist even Miss Gostrey: so grand is it not to
understand. He's wonderful."

"He is indeed," Strether conceded. "He
wouldn't tell me of this affair — only said he
had an engagement; but with such a gloom,
you must let me insist, as if it had been an engagement to be hanged. Then silently and secretly he turns up here with you. Do you call
*that* 'lasting'?"

"Oh I hope it's lasting!" Miss Barrace said.
"But he only, at the best, bears with me. He
doesn't understand — not one little scrap. He's
delightful. He's wonderful," she repeated.

"Michelangelesque!" — little Bilham completed her meaning. "He *is* a success. Moses, on
the ceiling, brought down to the floor, over-
whelming, colossal, but somehow portable."

"Certainly, if you mean by portable," she
returned, "looking so well in one's carriage.
He's too funny beside me in his corner; he
looks like somebody, somebody foreign and
famous, *en exil;* so that people wonder — it's
very amusing — whom I'm taking about. I
show him Paris, show him everything, and he
never turns a hair. He's like the Indian chief
one reads about, who, when he comes up to
Washington to see the Great Father, stands
wrapt in his blanket and gives no sign. *I* might
be the Great Father — from the way he takes
everything." She was delighted at this hit of
her identity with that personage — it fitted so
her character; she declared it was the title she
meant henceforth to adopt. "And the way he

sits, too, in the corner of my room, only looking at my visitors very hard and as if he wanted
to start something! They wonder what he does
want to start. But he's wonderful," Miss Barrace once more insisted. "He has never started
anything yet."

It presented him none the less, in truth, to
her actual friends, who looked at each other
in intelligence, with frank amusement on Bilham's part and a shade of sadness on Strether's.
Strether's sadness sprang — for the image had
its grandeur — from his thinking how little he
himself was wrapt in his blanket, how little, in
marble halls, all too oblivious of the Great Father, he resembled a really majestic aboriginal.
But he had also another reflexion. "You've all
of you here so much visual sense that you've
somehow all 'run' to it. There are moments
when it strikes one that you haven't any
other."

"Any moral," little Bilham explained,
watching serenely, across the garden, the several *femmes du monde*. "But Miss Barrace has
a moral distinction," he kindly continued;
speaking as if for Strether's benefit not less
than for her own.

"*Have* you?" Strether, scarce knowing what
he was about, asked of her almost eagerly.

"Oh not a distinction" — she was mightily
amused at his tone — "Mr. Bilham's too good.
But I think I may say a sufficiency. Yes, a sufficiency. Have you supposed strange things of
me?" — and she fixed him again, through all

her tortoise-shell, with the droll interest of it.
"You *are* all indeed wonderful. I should aw-
fully disappoint you. I do take my stand on my
sufficiency. But I know, I confess," she went
on, "strange people. I don't know how it happens; I don't do it on purpose; it seems to be
my doom — as if I were always one of their
habits: it's wonderful! I dare say moreover,"
she pursued with an interested gravity, "that I
do, that we all do here, run too much to mere
eye. But how can it be helped? We're all looking at each other — and in the light of Paris
one sees what things resemble. That's what the
light of Paris seems always to show. It's the
fault of the light of Paris — dear old light!"

"Dear old Paris!" little Bilham echoed.

"Everything, every one shows," Miss Barrace
went on.

"But for what they really are?" Strether
asked.

"Oh, I like your Boston 'reallys'! But sometimes — yes."

"Dear old Paris then!" Strether resignedly
sighed while for a moment they looked at
each other. Then he broke out: "Does Madame de Vionnet do that? I mean really show
for what she is?"

Her answer was prompt. "She's charming.
She's perfect."

"Then why did you a minute ago say 'Oh,
oh, oh!' at her name?"

She easily remembered. "Why, just because — ! She's wonderful."

"Ah she too?" — Strether had almost a groan.

But Miss Barrace had meanwhile perceived relief. "Why not put your question straight to the person who can answer it best?"

"No," said little Bilham; "don't put any question; wait, rather — it will be much more fun — to judge for yourself. He has come to take you to her."

In a form the very competitive play of which impinges directly on Strether's sensibility, this conversation enacts the "conversion" of things into art, the transformation of what is uninteresting, like the company of Waymarsh, into literary and artistic fantasy that is a spur to interest, wonder, and life. He is transformed, as is Gloriani by Strether, into an *objet d'art,* and then into a carnival figure: " 'He's wonderful,' she repeated. 'Michelangelesque!' — little Bilham completed her meaning." But "meaning" is not, of course, what concerns either of them so much as brilliance of inventiveness; Miss Barrace therefore tries immediately to top him with a description of Waymarsh as "the Indian chief one reads about, who, when he comes up to Washington to see the Great Father, stands wrapt in his blanket and gives no sign." Her being "delighted by this hit" indicates still further how social contact among these people is in the mode of an artistic performance. When Strether objects — "you've all of you here so much visual sense that you've somehow all 'run' to it. There are moments when it strikes one that you haven't any other" — it is immediately obvious that this degree of aggressive penetration is not characteristic of him at all. It belongs to

James and to his intentions in the whole novel, rather than to any characterization of power in Strether. Whatever impact Strether's remarks may have on the reader, they have little effect on Bilham, whose answer ("any moral") is delivered indifferently as he watches "serenely, across the garden, the several *femmes du monde.*" His casualness in this instance simply includes what Strether says without letting it modify the conditions, essentially visual ones, by which pleasure is not merely enjoyed but created.

The effect of this scene is of a beautiful and ecstatic generosity of response by which rather ordinary things are converted into wonders. And there could be nothing more trivial or degrading to what the novel offers at such points than to accuse Strether of illusions. Rather, the book makes us feel that his generosity has been betrayed by the materials — like Chad — on which it has expended itself. People really ought to try to live up to such an imagination of them as Strether's — that finally is what the book asks us to believe, not anything so tiresome as that Strether has failed to be in touch with reality. Of course he has — with the result that the novel can give us some of the most exalting beatifications of things and people anywhere in fiction. Because the novel celebrates the conversion of life into pleasure, most readings have failed from the persistent critical practice of translating that pleasure back into life (pleasure in that respect usually is an illusion, of course) or into sophisticated moralisms about Strether's failures to be involved more directly (imagination is thought to be a symptom of indirection) with other people.

And yet the novel is by no means epicurean — the moments of delight are especially vivid because they are grasped with a sort of astonishment at their availability. There is astonishment, too — one implicit with a Puritan morality of usefulness — that pleasure, delight, even the glories of art actually can mean so little and can have results of no practical consequence. Far from being merely satirized, therefore, the morality of Woollett exists as a crucial and invigorating pressure in the book. Perhaps one should say that the dignity of Woollett accrues to that form of its morality that James "converts" into his own. It is what allows him to write so often, and never more eloquently than here and in *The Golden Bowl,* about the heartbreaking *waste* of heightened human consciousness, the waste of art on the finally relentless ordinariness of daily life. In James, as in the Shakespeare of *King Lear,* the consciousness, developed by seeing the extremities of pleasure or pain, must simply be satisfied with itself. It cannot translate itself into anything else; it must rest within the "rightness" of the people who have it. There is no other environment for it.

The novel ends with a conversation between Strether and Maria Gostrey in which the word "right" holds in very fine equilibrium both a moral and an aesthetic meaning:

> "It isn't so much your *being* 'right' — it's your horrible sharp eye for what makes you so."
>
> "Oh but you're just as bad yourself. You can't resist me when I point that out."
>
> She sighed it at last all comically, all tragically, away. "I can't indeed resist you."
>
> "Then there we are!" said Strether.

The crucial words in the passage — "right," "Then there we are!" — carry with them a power derived from similar words or phrases used throughout the novel. We need only remember Strether's journey into the country in Book Eleven. Sitting for lunch at a garden's edge that almost overhangs the water, he sees the countryside as — one might say he "converts" it into — "a certain small Lambinet that had charmed him long years before at a Boston dealer's." All the "picture" needs for its perfection, he thinks, is the appearance of a boat coming down the stream. And,

> What he saw was exactly the right thing — a boat advancing round the bend and containing a man who held the paddles and a lady, at the stern, with a pink parasol. It was suddenly as if these figures, or something like them, had been wanted in the picture, had been wanted more or less all day, and had now drifted into sight, with the slow current, on purpose to fill up the measure.

With a quite obvious metaphoric implication, the boat soon begins to go "a little wild," to warp and distort the aesthetic perfection of which, for Strether, it was meant to be a part, to be "the right thing." The reason, simply, is that the boat holds Chad and Madame de Vionnet. Here, as earlier in the garden scene, and in the final encounter with Maria Gostrey, the hero must adjust his aesthetic vision of things to a reality which is instead eliciting his moral concern. Admirably, Strether can almost at once, and with some degree of pleasure, recognize that there have been benefits to him, to Chad, to Madame de Vionnet, to life itself, in the simplicity that

let him think the lovers have had only a "virtuous attachment." His simplicity has to some degree been
nearly contemptible — he has viewed his friends, we are
told, "as a little girl might have dressed her doll." But it
has also made him open to a variety of impressions that
will sustain him not only after his discovery of the lovers, but also, we are made to feel, after the conclusion of
the novel.

Strether's own sense of "rightness," of being inescapably what he is, gets expressed at the end not plaintively
but with the exhilarated energy of his assertion: "Then
there we are!" However much he can "convert" life into
art and thereby enhance the existence of others, and his
own, he knows that he cannot himself be "converted"
into a different creature. Self-awareness as a form of limitation, without the meanness that projects those limitations onto the lives of others, emanates beautifully and
poignantly from Strether's thoughts as he lunches with
Madame de Vionnet:

> He had at that time gathered them in, the ex-
> planations — he had stored them up; but it was
> at present as if he had either soared above or
> sunk below them — he couldn't tell which; he
> could somehow think of none that didn't seem
> to leave the appearance of collapse and cyni-
> cism easier for him than lucidity. How could
> he wish it to be lucid for others, for any one,
> that he, for the hour, saw reasons enough in
> the mere way the bright clean ordered water-
> side life came in at the open window? — the
> mere way Madame de Vionnet, opposite him
> over their intensely white table-linen, their

*omelette aux tomates,* their bottle of straw-colored Chablis, thanked him for everything almost with the smile of a child, while her grey eyes moved in and out of their talk, back to the quarter of the warm spring air, in which early summer had already begun to throb, and then back again to his face and their human questions.

How could he wish here to be "lucid" for others any more than in the garden scene he could have spoken to anyone of his impressions without "appearing to talk nonsense"? The response is to the "mere way" in which lunch is given at this particular time and place. And this luncheon elucidates the final one, the pattern being itself a suggestion of the delights for Strether in that most solipsistic of pleasures, eating. That Strether cannot wish to be "lucid for others" about what is happening, gives a special dimension to his otherwise priggish statement, at that final meeting, that his only logic is "not out of the whole affair to have got anything for myself." The Puritanical rigor in the remark derives from Woollett, but the phrase also calls to mind the necessary discontinuities so pronounced in American literature between the visionary and the actual possession of things. What Strether means is that nothing, certainly not marriage to Maria Gostrey, could make lucid, could represent his inward state. Food can therefore serve his imagination as well as even Paris can — both *are* what he makes of them. Now alienated not only from Woollett but also from Paris, Strether can husband his impressions of both places.

Necessarily, this heightened vision of "the mere way

of doing things" involves an indifference to sexual
liaison. One "lucidity" of lunch with Madame de Vionnet might have been that he should want to make love
to her, want to possess her as a fitting summation of
his imaginative, if not his digestive possession of their
*"omelette aux tomates,* their bottle of straw-colored
Chablis." Later, when Maria Gostrey seems to offer
herself to him ("You've excited *me. I'm* distinctly rest-
less"), he claims that "I'm not in harmony with what
surrounds me. You *are.* I take it too hard." In part
he means that in the palpable world he looks like a kind
of fool, but James allows at once for significances more
specific and also less solemn. Interspersed with his remarks are the details that he is "leaning back in his
chair," surely not a sign of unrelaxed discomfort with
his surroundings, with "his eyes on a small, ripe, round
melon," an indication that here, as in the lunch with
Madame de Vionnet, he does have a harmony with those
physical attributes of the scene that nourish and stimulate him while themselves remaining passive, like still
lives. What he gives back to the world is his imagination
of it; what he keeps wholly to himself is his body.

*The Ambassadors* is superior to *The Blithedale Romance* mostly because it is a loving book in which
Strether's limitations burst forth in the directions
opened by James's excitement and compassion. Gloriani's garden, the various balcony scenes, the little
luncheon scenes — all allow otherwise pathetic qualities
in the hero to express themselves with an energy and an
oddity of life that make them indelible. Their detailed
glamor is James's way of saying that the creative imagination is finally responsible not for what it receives from
reality but for the reality it creates. Hawthorne never

dares admit in his characterization of Coverdale that perhaps self-enhancement isn't the only result of living imaginatively off the lives of others. The result can also be a gift to the general human consciousness, represented by the reader, of what life *might* be. James is apt to strike many young readers of these times as intensely more exciting and contemporary than Hawthorne because he does manage to protect the imagination of pleasure from almost all moral and social categories, including "sex." But he also shows how the occasion for these delights is made possible by the residual if dying power of these categories. Like *La Dame aux camélias,* with which the novel has interesting similarities of plot, *The Ambassadors* is a work in which we are charmed and excited out of moral attitudes without which none of that charm and excitement could have come to us.

*The Ambassadors* succeeds in freeing itself from the old-fashioned questions that critics still ask about it, questions about motive and fulfillment derived from novels shaped by conventional moralities. Necessarily there is an echo here of the Aesthetic Movement of the 1890's, regardless of James's impatient remarks about Pater, and an anticipation, too, of the current resurgence of that movement. Art conceived as an activity rather than as a product is now, as before, a direct challenge to those who believe in the fixed realities of our physical environment or our moral life. That Hawthorne should be even tangentially connected with this development is remarkable in view of the drab way in which most critics, including James, have talked about his deprivations.

The connection between Strether and Coverdale is of

a significance greater than anything it tells us about the relationship of Hawthorne and James. Coverdale the poet, Strether the man who is busy "converting" life into artistic still lifes, illustrate the fact that an indifference to social reality, even a solipsistic one, is not to be taken as a sign that such characters or their creators are socially deprived. Quite the reverse. They retreat from society into a sort of aesthetic dandyism. No such retreat, we shall now see, was available to Huck Finn and no imagination of such a retreat was possible for Mark Twain.

# IV
## Transatlantic Configurations: Mark Twain and Jane Austen

> To me his [Poe's] prose is unreadable — like Jane Austin's [sic]. No, there is a difference. I could read his prose on salary, but not Jane's. Jane is entirely impossible. It seems a great pity that they allowed her to die a natural death.
>
> MARK TWAIN, Letter to Howells, January 18, 1909

> Just that one omission alone [of Jane Austen's novels from a ship's library] would make a fairly good library out of a library that hadn't a book in it.
>
> MARK TWAIN, *Following the Equator*

Like some of Hawthorne's better stories, *Huckleberry Finn* takes literary advantage of the complaints enunciated earlier by Emerson and Cooper: that not only American writing but also American social life was subservient to conventions, especially literary ones, that prevented the development of new human possibilities. A kindred awareness enters English fiction only with George Eliot and, with consequences for the shape of fiction, with Lawrence and Joyce. But in the nineteenth century, the note is most emphatically struck in American rather than in English fiction. The element in Cooper, Hawthorne, Melville, Mark Twain, and Henry James that anticipates *Ulysses* and *Women in Love* is the recognition that society provides an environment that in fact merely imitates the images provided by fiction. To accept what society calls "real" or "natural" thus became for American novelists such as these the equivalent of subscribing to the literary conventions from which they often claim to be liberating their readers. The problem provides the actual substance and meaning of Hawthorne's "The Maypole of Merrymount," where allegory and pastoral, in the forms of revelers and Puritans, are said to "contend for empire" and for control, by the way, of the destiny of the young lovers. Society in *Huckleberry Finn* is similarly a tissue of bookish assumptions and artificial forms that its members take for reality itself.

American writers of the nineteenth century took novels very seriously, showing in this, too, more kinship to twentieth-century writers than to their English contemporaries of the nineteenth. Novels for them were capable not simply of offering entertainment or of making protests against social ills. Living as they did in a society so anxious for models of social manners and sophistication, they felt that English fiction might actually shape the reality of American life and behavior. Thus Mark Twain's comments on Jane Austen represent more than an effort to bait William Dean Howells, her most distinguished American defender, or to suggest that another of James Fenimore Cooper's literary offenses was his first novel, *Precaution,* presumably an imitation of Jane Austen's *Persuasion.* Though he is too contemptuous to explain in any detail why he dislikes her, it can be inferred that he shared the more substantial criticisms made by Emerson and Henry James. Taken together, their reactions to Jane Austen represent a significant American dissatisfaction with the kind of social ordering of existence that takes place in her novels. The social organizations of which her novels are an image are inhospitable to the romantic and

aspiring characters admired, with some differences, by
her American critics. Emerson, with his well-known distaste for what he calls "novels of costume," found Jane
Austen "vulgar in tone, sterile in invention, imprisoned
in the wretched conventions of English society, without
genius, wit, or knowledge of the world. Never was life so
pinched and narrow," he continues in his journal of
August 5, 1861, and her only subject, "marriageableness," is dismissed, with an ill-used quotation from
Byron, as the " 'nympholepsy of a fond despair,' say,
rather, of an English boarding house. Suicide," he concludes, "is more respectable." About forty-five years
later, Henry James, who had learned many lessons from
her, complained in an address given in Philadelphia,
that her popularity, whipped up by "the stiff breeze of
the commercial" ("Their 'dear,' our dear, everybody's
dear Jane"), was in part due to

> the extraordinary grace of her facility, in
> fact of her unconsciousness; as if, at the most,
> for difficulty, for embarrassment, she some-
> times, over her work basket, her tapestry flow-
> ers, in the spare, cool drawing room of other
> days, fell a-musing, lapsed too metaphorically,
> as one may say, into wool gathering, and her
> dropped stitches, of these pardonable, of these
> precious moments, were afterwards picked up
> as little touches of human truth, little glimpses
> of steady vision, little master strokes of imagi-
> nation.

It is as hard here, as in *Hawthorne,* not to think that
the critic is being overmastered by the self-aggrandizing
entertainer. His condescensions are most pronounced

when he is discussing English and American writers with whom he has some literary or intellectual affinities.\* A decade or so earlier, when it came to a criticism of Emerson, he could observe that the possible explanations for other vagaries of Emerson's literary taste "still leaves his indifference to Cervantes and Miss Austen unaccounted for." Shift around as he might, the negative side of his ambivalence toward Jane Austen is finally very much like Emerson's unmoderated criticism: she lacks inclusiveness. In the last important comments he was to make about her, he allows the issue to be raised by an unmistakably rhetorical question: "Why shouldn't it be argued against her," it is asked in "The New Novel," "that where her testimony complacently ends, the pressure of our appetite presumes exactly to begin?"

More than any other novelist in English, Jane Austen is supremely confident that the appetite of her audience as well as of her characters can be satisfied by social unions, especially by marriage. It is not surprising that Emerson, Mark Twain, and Henry James should find "the pressure of appetite" unsatisfied. Despite the many differences among them, they all tend to see a necessary division between a part of us expressed by accommodations to social systems, and another, more admirable, even if impractical part, that exists in the imagination

---

\* James was never to admire even *Huckleberry Finn*, and as late as 1907 he asserts that Mark Twain would contribute "a clarionet solo only" to the composite novel, *The Whole Family*, being planned by Miss Elizabeth Jackson. (Mark Twain declined the invitation.) On his side, Mark Twain in 1885 would rather have been "damned to John Bunyan's heaven" than read *The Bostonians*, which ran serially in *Century* along with a section of *Huckleberry Finn*. But in a letter in 1900 he had come to the point of calling James "a master."

only, or in a vocabulary of abstractions, or in relationships to landscape. Emerson has suffered from a general modern naïveté about romantic writers — the assumption that they are not aware of the incompatibility of many of their images with social and physical realities and with the inescapable pressures of time. Emerson was explicitly and eloquently aware of these tensions and of their result in what he called "doubleness." Huck Finn will later worry about "playing double," and to read Emerson with such novels in mind as the Leather-Stocking series, *Huckleberry Finn, The Portrait of a Lady,* or even *The Ambassadors,* where social artifice is given some positive definitions, is to come upon passages that describe the problem faced by the leading characters in these books and by their creators. The problem is that at some point, usually at the end, the heroes and heroines tend to escape definition in the social or even psychological terms on which, only to a lesser extent than in *Emma,* the novels themselves have depended. The eccentricities in the structure of *Huckleberry Finn* and in many of James's novels are thus symptoms of some larger distrust of social structures themselves. Emerson's phrasing is relevant to such works precisely because it is so general. Generality and vagueness are necessary attributes of all that is opposed to the fixed, publicly accredited reality of things as they are. Emerson's language is, if anything, less vague, less general, however, than most explanations of why, say, Huck must at the end of his novel "light out for the Territory" or why, at the end of hers, Isabel Archer must return to Rome. For Emerson,

> The worst feature of this double consciousness
> is, that the two lives, of the understanding and

of the soul, which we lead, really show very little relation to each other; never meet and measure each other: one prevails now, all buzz and din; and the other prevails then, all infinitude and paradise; and, with the progress of life, the two discover no greater disposition to reconcile themselves. Yet, what is my faith? What am I? What but a thought of serenity and independence, an abode in the deep blue sky? Presently the clouds shut down again; yet we retain the belief that this pretty web we weave will at last be overshot and reticulated with veins of the blue, and that the moments will characterize the days. Patience, then, is for us, is it not? Patience, and still patience. When we pass, as we presently shall, into some new infinitude, out of this Iceland of negations, it will please us to reflect that though we had few virtues or consolations, we bore with our indigence, nor once strove to repair it with hypocrisy or false heat of any kind.

To claim that one can be a "thought of serenity and independence" is to claim the "freedom" imagined and lost in *Huckleberry Finn,* in Melville, above all in James, who is obsessed with the term. But praise of "patience," with such stoical iteration and even with a kind of pathetic call for reassurance — "Patience, then, is for us, is it not? Patience, and still patience" — is a recognition that there are in this life no very permanent lodgings in "the deep blue sky," at James's Gardencourt, or on the raft. Emerson's romanticism is the more impressive because, like James's, it is meant to relieve rather than merely elude the tensions of existence. Both insist,

as William James was also to do, that to lack faith or belief is to be the reverse of worldly and practical, and that
despite any contrary immediate evidence there are ultimate, practical benefits to the self from an active commitment to ideals. "This pretty web we weave will at
last," Emerson persists in hoping, "be overshot and
reticulated with veins of the blue." Such a hope, and not
merely the "freedom" promised by death, turns "patience" into a form of action, of evolution.

The illusion that society might someday, somehow be
transformed by the vision and sacrifice of an Isabel
Archer or the needs of a Huck Finn is necessarily among
the things that their creators try to make the reader believe even when they themselves are skeptical. It is part
of the suspense, part of the beguilement, part even of
the entertainment of fiction. The humor of Huck's
narrative voice, the youthful glamor of Isabel's pro-
nouncements in *The Portrait of a Lady,* the very ingenu-
ousness of which makes us feel an amused tenderness for
her — these result from styles meant to sustain us past
the glowerings of our own knowledge about probable
failure. Thereby, we can share in the nostalgic regret
when the failures do occur, as if for a lost possibility.
There is no better description of how we should read
novels of this kind than that provided by Emerson, for
whom the act of reading was itself an exercise of "double consciousness": "An imaginative book," he remarks
in "The Poet," "renders us more service at first, by stim-
ulating us through its tropes, than afterwards when we
arrive at the precise sense of the author."

The problem for a novelist like James or Mark Twain
is that the tropes by which they stimulate us cannot represent merely "abodes in the deep blue sky." They more

often represent things in the realm of matter, like Gatsby's beautiful shirts, things that belong emphatically to those worldly aspects of social life which are often the enemy of "freedom." Thus, even should a character decide that he is really a "thought of serenity and independence," he generally discovers himself insisting on this within social relations that thwart his independence. Emerson's "I" could not exist in a novel at all — he simply would not be interested in social dialogue for a sufficient length of time. As a result, even novels full of Emersonian inclinations, like *The Portrait of a Lady* or *Huckleberry Finn,* must render life outside the imagination of the hero in a way that endows it, however meretriciously, with the promise of "freedom," "infinitude," and "serenity." The reader is made to feel this promise, embedded in the very things that are to defeat it, to an extent that makes him at least recognize why the hero might be deceived. Meanwhile, there is a simultaneous effort, a very obvious one in *Huckleberry Finn,* to include the author and reader in a delayed action, so to speak, at once of knowledge and silence, against the innocence of the hero, and above all against the fact that he only partly recognizes society — all that is other than himself except landscape — for what it is: "a conspiracy," as Emerson would have it, "against the manhood of every one of its members . . . a joint-stock company." In *Huckleberry Finn* it is a stock company of another sort, a kind of theatrical troupe; and in James it is often a conspiracy of self-interest that has all the charm of sophisticated manners.

Needless to say the attitudes of Mark Twain and Henry James may be similar but could not be identical. For James social manners and even deviousness were

sometimes not a sign of social conformity but the necessary technique for escaping it. Style, in the broadest
sense, became a kind of defense against moralistic and
sociological judgments and presuppositions, judgments
that society is always ready to make of its members. By
contrast, Mark Twain was emotionally committed to a
particular form of society in which he had spent his
youth. Imaginary alternatives for him could never be
more than gratuitous fantasy. When he does head in the
direction of fantasy after *Huckleberry Finn,* with
*Pudd'nhead Wilson* and *The Mysterious Stranger,* it is
toward a saturnalia of social repudiation. *Huckleberry
Finn* is more complicated than anything in James before
*The Bostonians* because of Mark Twain's affection for a
character whose longings are a curious blend of Isabel
Archer's dream of "freedom" and Mark Twain's own
nostalgic desire for community. The relatively simple
dichotomy in the early James between the imagination
of freedom and the facts of social life that ultimately kill
it is in *Huckleberry Finn* a struggle within a character
who is not even conscious of the issues as Isabel Archer
would abstractly define them.

The struggle within Huck is the more interesting because there is evidence in the book that Mark Twain has
already resolved a similar struggle in himself. It is made
apparent, even in the first chapter of *Huckleberry Finn,*
that society in any institutionalized form is merely the
projection of the fantasies, generally derived from literature, both of children and adults. As a result, there is a
"double consciousness" operating in the very modes of
presentation: Huck's socially anxious voice never carries
fully the implications of social contempt and rejection

that govern the metaphorical pattern of the book. When Huck does move, after the offense and apology to Jim in Chapters xv and xvi, toward recognitions equivalent to his creator's, the dramatic organization of the novel, which depends on the social audibility of Huck's voice, first totters and then collapses. When, by contrast, the heroine of *Emma* moves toward social awarenesses equivalent to Jane Austen's, she begins to speak more directly and naturally, most like the plain-speaking and forthright Knightley, and is prepared for the "perfect happiness of the union" which is announced at the end of the novel.

In part, the objections to Jane Austen by Mark Twain and American writers of roughly similar prejudice can be explained as a blindness to society as she imagines it. Their prejudice gets between even these illustrious readers and what in fact the work of Jane Austen does express about society and artifice. They are unable to see, so alien to them is her positive vision of social experience, that she is fully aware of the dangers *in* society which for them are the dangers *of* it. The capacity to imagine society as including the threat of conformity and artificiality and as offering, nevertheless, beneficial opportunities for self-discovery is seldom evident in Emerson, and is in Mark Twain mostly in works before *Huckleberry Finn* and inferior to it.

By contrast, Jane Austen is always aware that the possible form of society in *Emma* — and the form is fluid and self-creating to a degree never allowed in *Huckleberry Finn* — might easily be determined by Mrs. Elton, with her preposterous affectations, by Mr. Weston, with his good-hearted indiscriminateness, or even by the type of old Mr. Woodhouse, who is "never able to suppose people different from himself." The enclosure of natural vitality within a social situation that threatens to smother it is rendered with Jane Austen's characteristic suggestion that the state of any social gathering is measurable by the condition of social dialogue. One evidence of the relatively uncomplicated feeling of American writers about the possibilities of such social meetings is the remarkable deficiency of dialogue, both in quantity and in quality, in such American novelists as Cooper, Hawthorne, or Dreiser. Conversation as an index of a society is brilliantly manipulated by Jane Austen in all her works but I think nowhere as effectively as in *Emma,* during the scene at the Woodhouse's to celebrate the visit from London of John and Isabella Knightley. It offers a comic illustration of how irredeemably dull even an exceptional evening in *Emma* can be. The positive standards against which the dullness is measured are defined at the beginning of the chapter and in terms that relate the scene to other crucial moments in the novel and finally to Box Hill. The assured alternative to tedium evoked at the beginning makes the subsequent dullness comic and lovable rather than tedious. Significantly, this alternative can display itself not when the whole group gathers but only before that, when Emma and Knightley are alone. In Jane Austen, as later in Forster and Lawrence, the best society is not a group but a pair — such is the English discrimination against both gregariousness and mere self-communion. Before the whole group assembles, the conversation of Knightley and Emma can sparkle with intelligence and unforced wit, with discriminations wholly missing from the more general conversation that will follow:

. . . she hoped it might rather assist the restoration of friendship, that when he came into the room she had one of the children with her — the youngest, a nice little girl about eight months old, who was now making her first visit to Hartfield, and very happy to be danced about in her aunt's arms. It did assist; for though he began with grave looks and short questions, he was soon led on to talk of them all in the usual way, and to take the child out of her arms with all the unceremoniousness of perfect amity. Emma felt they were friends again; and the conviction giving her at first great satisfaction, and then a little sauciness, she could not help saying, as he was admiring the baby,

"What a comfort it is, that we think alike about our nephews and nieces. As to men and women, our opinions are sometimes very different; but with regard to these children, I observe we never disagree."

"If you were as much guided by nature in your estimate of men and women, and as little under the power of fancy and whim in your dealings with them, as you are where these children are concerned, we might always think alike."

"To be sure — our discordancies must always arise from my being in the wrong."

"Yes," said he, smiling — "and reason good. I was sixteen years old when you were born."

"A material difference then," she replied — "and no doubt you were much my superior in judgment at that period of our lives; but does not the lapse of one-and-twenty years bring our understanding a good deal nearer?"

"Yes — a good deal *nearer*."

"But still, not near enough to give me a chance of being right, if we think differently."

"I still have the advantage of you by sixteen years' experience."

. . . "I only want to know [she said] that Mr. Martin is not very, very bitterly disappointed."

"A man cannot be more so," was his short, full answer.

"Ah! — Indeed I am very sorry. — Come, shake hands with me."

This had just taken place and with great cordiality, when John Knightley made his appearance, and "How d'ye do, George?" and "John, how are you?" succeeded in true English style, burying under a calmness that seemed all but indifference, the real attachment which would have led either of them, if requisite, to do everything for the good of the other.

The "unceremoniousness of perfect amity" describes the ideal social arrangement as Jane Austen imagines it. It describes society ("amity") divested of artificiality, of fancy and whim, which are the enemies of "nature" in Jane Austen as much as are forms of them in *Huckleberry Finn* — tricks, games, and art. "Unceremoniousness" as a condition of unaffected social harmony is apparent in the charming directness of Emma's invita-

tion to "Come, shake hands with me," and in the
equally economical greeting of the brothers, described
in terms applicable to some larger consideration of what
is natural in social unions. The encouragement to gen-
eralization is given in Jane Austen's allusion to "the
true English style." The weight of the phrase betrays, to
me, a slightly bothersome anxiety on Jane Austen's part
to give a dimension to the scene larger than it inherently deserves. Such self-consciously patriotic definitions
are the result, very likely, of an anticipated threat to the
"true English style." The threat does not, at this point
in the novel, have its source in Frank Churchill's or
Mrs. Elton's fabricated giddiness, but rather in an
equally debilitating social drabness that is about to de-
scend on the gathering. Emma is a silent witness to the
"two natural divisions" in the conversation when the
whole group is involved — of the Knightley brothers,
who discuss land and farming, and of Isabelle and her
father, who discuss the weather and gruel. When Emma
does join in this talk, it is in a heroic effort, too lengthy
in development to be quoted here, to heal not the "natural" but the conscious and asserted division that results
from Mr. Woodhouse's criticism of his son-in-law's housing arrangements in London.

The moment is indicative of the degree to which
"amity" in Jane Austen depends on the observance of
"natural" divisions, rather than on social class, and on
discriminations and human choices that can significantly modify class structure, as in the hints that accompany
Knightley's admiration for Mr. Martin. Any conscious
effort either to erect barriers or to lower them results
always in Jane Austen in some form of nastiness. Very
often the nastiness comes from Jane Austen herself in

her observations of characters who are moved close to
the reader from a safe distance where they had been
relatively anonymous. Isabella, for example, having been
at first described as a "pretty, elegant little woman, of
gentle manners, and a disposition remarkably amiable,"
emerges from this scene, a few pages later, as something
of a fool. The narrator, like Emma herself and like the
reader, is always in some such tentative, even tempera-
mental relation to other people in the novel. Up close,
Isabella's conversation proves hilariously vapid and repetitious, and Jane Austen's exasperation is made clear by
her final reference to her as merely "the daughter." The
view of a character in Jane Austen's novels can be
benign and generally favorable as long as he stays in the
area separated by a "natural division" from the more
exacting, quick, vitally differentiating region inhabited
by Emma, Knightley, Jane Austen, and the reader. The
operative concept here, crucial to an understanding of
this and all her works, is expressed by the term "amiable."

The term is used, we have just seen, of Isabella, and it
is applied also to Harriet, Mr. Weston, Mrs. Weston,
Elton, and most of the other characters in the novel. It
is typical of Jane Austen that she should reveal her own
position not through a multiplication of terms but
through careful siftings among the various interpreta-
tions of a particular word. In this instance, the range of
meanings is extraordinarily wide, and the term itself is a
metaphor for the several kinds of social "amity," both
good and disreputable, that are given expression in this
novel. What is permitted here is what is denied in
*Huckleberry Finn* and, for the most part, in James's
novels — a choice of strictly social alternatives. Knightley provides, as he often does, the proper way to think

about a term used by everyone else with uncritical liberality. He is discussing Frank Churchill, whom Emma has just called "amiable":

> "No, Emma, your amiable young man can be amiable only in French, not in English. He may be very 'aimable,' have very good manners, and be very agreeable; but he can have no English delicacy towards the feelings of other people: nothing really amiable about him."

In objecting to the importation of foreign styles into native speech and manner, Jane Austen is apparently no less decisive than Mark Twain himself. "English" amiableness involves "the delicacy towards the feelings of other people" exhibited by Emma in her efforts to moderate differences even though, as in the scene just discussed, she herself takes no interest in the issues. A lack of such delicacy takes the form not merely of being artificial — "French" — but also of being like Mr. Woodhouse ("never being able to suppose that other people could be different from himself") or like Mr. Weston, who also ignores "differences" in his efforts to bring people together in "general friendship," as Emma disparagingly calls it. Oddly, their forms of doltish "amiability" become, on inspection, very much like the French "aimable," resembling Frank Churchill's stylish manners which are also used impersonally and with everyone, without taking account of "differences" or of the particular "feelings of others."

We can guess that Mark Twain would appreciate Emma's difficulties in escaping a social life often as "dismal regular and decent" as life for Huck at the Widow Douglas's. Emma's response to one sort of "amiableness"

— the tedium of bland conviviality — often encourages her to another form of it, to "amiable" relations with imaginary versions of other people. Like Huck, under similar circumstances, she play-acts or "stretches." Threatened with a loss of her individuality through gregariousness, she is apt to lose it to fantasies that equally distort her true and natural relationships to those around her.

By trying at such times to reform society in her imagination — to create, like an American hero, a new environment for herself — Emma necessarily becomes selfconscious about social class; her sententiousness at such points is worthy of the social-climbing Mrs. Elton. In her efforts to elevate Harriet Smith, for instance, Emma's affectation of speech is only the first evidence of how close she can come to a form of dialogue — and therefore a form of social life — of which the Eltons are the grotesque examples. We can actually listen to this process when Emma discusses Harriet with the still un-married Elton. They talk about taking a "likeness" of Harriet, an indication of their difficulty in seeing her accurately. We can hear Emma slowly losing with Elton the voice we have heard in her conversation with Knightley. There is a contrast between her customarily crisp, cheerfully bitchy tone, much like Jane Austen's at the end of this passage, and, preceding it, a conversation in which the rhythms of her speech become synchro-nized ("Skilful has been the hand," "Great has been the pleasure") with the flattery of Elton's:

> "I am glad you think I have been useful to
> her; but Harriet only wanted drawing out, and
> receiving a few, very few hints. She had all the

natural grace and sweetness of temper and art-
lessness in herself. I have done very little."

"If it were admissible to contradict a lady,"
said the gallant Mr. Elton —

"I have perhaps given her a little more decision of character, have taught her to think on
points which had not fallen in her way before."

"Exactly so; that is what principally strikes
me. So much super-added decision of character! Skilful has been the hand."

"Great has been the pleasure, I am sure. I
never met with a disposition more truly amiable."

"I have no doubt of it." And it was spoken
with a sort of sighing animation, which had a
vast deal of the lover.

Emma is surrounded with provocations to create for
herself, through a kind of language which she will later
mock, a world of theatrical possibility. Yet in this case
the fancied world turns out, in the deadening repetitiveness of "indeeds" and "exactly so's," to have the
verbal features of the world of unmannered dullness
inhabited by Mr. Woodhouse, Isabella, or Miss Bates.
By contrast, extravagance of language in Cooper or
Melville is often an indication of a character's liberation
from the confinements of socially accepted speech, a way
of extending and enriching his potentialities. All such
extensions in Jane Austen indicate not that a character
wants to remove himself from social artificialities which,
in her fashion, she dislikes as much as do Cooper or
Melville. Instead, they represent a drift toward eccen-

tricity. Taking the contrast to American fiction a bit
further, Emma and Harriet are a satiric version of those
pairs of characters in American fiction whose relationship has so little warrant in social custom as to be, for
some critics, sexually irregular. Such a treatment of
Huck and Jim has now become part of the standard
"case" about the book, but Mr. Fiedler's view represents, as I've already suggested, not a new penetration of
this or other American novels so much as a misapplica-
tion to them of standards that belong to the English novel
of manners. The tendency to separate oneself from society and to form relationships that flout established social
hierarchies is given a heroic pathos in American fiction,
while a similar tendency on the part of Jane Austen's
heroine is seen more mundanely as perhaps a good sign
— the girl has spirit — but as essentially rather silly.

The result of Emma's attempt to gain public acceptance of her fantasies about Harriet Smith is that she confuses everyone about their relationship to Harriet. They
forget to treat her with that "English delicacy towards
the feelings of other people" which is the best form of
"amiable" social relationship. Poor Harriet is so absorbed into Emma's fantasies that at some point she will
need, brutally, to be reminded of her natural place, just
as Emma is so reminded by Elton's shocked and nasty
response to the news that Emma intended Harriet and
not herself as his wife. No one can see Harriet clearly or
do a proper job of characterizing her. Emma cannot
take an accurate "likeness" of her ("You have made her
too tall," says Knightley), and because of Emma's dis-
tortions even Knightley cannot see Harriet with his
usual clarity. He can praise her at the beginning of
Chapter VII, when it seems she will find her proper

place as the wife of Martin, and then, within two pages, rather meanly criticize her for thinking, with Emma's encouragement, that she is of a station too high for such a marriage.

But if distortion of character is what threatens Harriet Smith, a name that does nothing to save her from anonymity, it is Emma herself who is most endangered. In this respect her position is again like Huck's when he chooses to sacrifice his own style in order to imitate Tom Sawyer, himself the embodiment of imitated "style." *Emma* is altogether more optimistic, however, about the heroine's lapses into "imitation." Jane Austen's satire has behind it a confidence that English society gives everyone a chance, as the society in *Huckleberry Finn* does not, to find a place that can be called "natural." The loss of "self-command," to use Emma's phrase, and the grotesqueness of self-expression that results from it is always accompanied in this novel by some kind of artificiality in relationships — through consciousness of rank, through mannered ways of addressing other people, through a gregariousness that ignores individual differences. All of these are opposed to the "amiableness" preferred by Knightley and defined by him as "English," the kind that requires a sensitivity to "differences," and therefore actually protects people like Harriet from being the victim of standards they cannot meet or from being exploited in the interest of other people's fancies. Knightley's definition of "amiableness," with its specific application to Churchill, is thus one of the dominant chords in the many that come to their fullest and most inclusive orchestration at Box Hill.

Jane Austen's achievement in the scene at Box Hill

can be measured by reading the end of it without re-
membering, for a moment, its connections to some of
the patterns that take shape in earlier chapters. What, it
might be asked, is all the excitement about? Emma has,
after all, in a moment of flightiness, only made a
thoughtless remark to garrulous old Miss Bates. And
when she does so, no one except Miss Bates and Knightley himself seem even to notice it. Why, then, after his
reprimand at the end of the picnic, should Miss Austen
be allowed the melodramatic claim that

> Never had she felt so agitated, mortified,
> grieved, at any circumstance in her life. She was
> most forcibly struck. The truth of his repre-
> sentation there was no denying. She felt it at
> her heart. How could she have been so brutal,
> so cruel to Miss Bates! — How could she have
> exposed herself to such ill opinion in any one
> she valued! And how suffer him to leave her
> without saying one word of gratitude, of con-
> currence, of common kindness.
>
> Time did not compose her. As she reflected
> more, she seemed but to feel it more. She
> never had been so depressed.

Anyone anxious to defend Jane Austen must wonder
here if she is not asking us to care too much — by excla-
mations, by the pained inquisitiveness of "How,"
"how," "And how" — about matters relatively trivial.
Mightn't it legitimately be asked at this point by Mark
Twain or Henry James if her notions of "grief" and
"mortification" are not as superficial as is the meaning
assigned in all her novels to the term "evil"? Such ques-

tions are made irrelevant as soon as we notice how the
language of the scene reshapes details from the rest of
the novel into a vision of English life and society. The
mastery by which Jane Austen can expand the significance of a particular moment even while keeping us
solidly within the minutiae of the occasion is rare in
fiction, though *Huckleberry Finn* will offer another instance. The echoes and parallels that occur in the scene
at Box Hill direct us back to the earlier scene between
Elton and Emma in which we hear her losing her voice
to his, to the scene of the evening with Isabella and John
Knightley, over gruel, in which the problem of forced
unity and "natural division" in a social gathering is
first dramatically defined, to the preparation for the
picnic in the immediately preceding chapter, where
Emma comments on the unfavorable aspects of Weston's
"unmanageable good will," and finally to an earlier
scene with Frank Churchill, Emma, and Mrs. Weston,
in which we hear Frank, as we have heard Elton, sounding like a man on stage, play-acting with a self-indul-
gence and conviviality that ignores the feelings and
identities of the people he addresses. He is also being
oblivious to the feelings of Jane Fairfax, whose expectations of his visit must compete with his illusion that
Emma wants him to remain with her:

> "Me! I should be quite in the way. But, per-
> haps — I may be equally in the way here. Miss
> Woodhouse looks as if she did not want me.
> My aunt always sends me off when she is shop-
> ping. She says I fidget her to death; and Miss
> Woodhouse looks as if she could almost say the
> same. What am I to do?"

"I am here on no business of my own," said
Emma, "I am only waiting for my friend. She
will probably have soon done, and then we
shall go home. But you had better go with
Mrs. Weston and hear the instrument."

"Well — if you advise it. — But (with a
smile) if Col. Campbell should have employed
a careless friend, and if it should prove to have
an indifferent tone — what shall I say? I shall
be no support to Mrs. Weston. She might do
very well by herself. A disagreeable truth
would be palatable through her lips, but I am
the wretchedest being in the world at a civil
falsehood."

"I do not believe any such thing," replied
Emma, — "I am persuaded that you can be as
insincere as your neighbours, when it is necessary . . ."

The reader's reaction to Frank here need not depend
entirely on Emma's tart comment about his insincerity.
He would in any case take her remark as playful, which
it is intended to be only in part. The style of the book
— he sounds at times like Elton, "exactly so" — has made
us alert to the offensive element in his play-acting. His
tone is unctuous, he is easy with words and with people,
while Emma, who can be equally adept in conversation,
speaks with precision and animation. She is quickened
by the play of specific personalities, while he is aware
less of the two women — he alludes to them in the third
person as if actually addressing the reader and not them

— than of the occasion they offer for a performance; there is even the hint of a stage direction in the parenthesized "(with a smile)."

Churchill is the logical villain of Box Hill, the man who brings into this pastoral setting, where the whole community is represented, the element of theater, of artificial amiability. The party is already wanting in communal feeling because of his father's forced breeding of fellowship between Emma's group and Mrs. Elton's. The "want of union" announced in the opening paragraph of the scene is thus a consequence of one sort of indiscriminate amiability that will lead, as it has before in Emma's experience, to another more dangerous form, and thence to a gross violation of the "English amiability" defined in Knightley's criticism of the "French" manners of Churchill.

"At first," we are told, "it was downright dullness to Emma," a sentence that is by now a warning of her susceptibility to imaginative flight beyond the social group, the potential dullness of which has before led to the "whim" and "fancy" of her relationship with Harriet Smith. Emma's gradual adoption of a role fabricated for her by Frank Churchill is, like everything else in this novel, subtle and unemphatic in presentation. When Frank starts to amuse her, she is flattered enough to feel "gay and easy," a bit later to be "gay and thoughtless," and still later, as she enters more fully into his game, her expression has become so remote from her true feelings that she "laughed because she was disappointed." Jane Austen's clarity about her own intentions is apparent in the subsequent dialogue, and it is characteristic that these intentions should be revealed dramatically, as part of a conversation among characters. To Churchill's excuse that his loss of temper the day before was due to the heat, Emma replies teasingly that

> "It is hotter to-day."
> "Not to my feelings. I am perfectly comfortable today."
> "You are comfortable because you are under command."
> "Your command? — Yes."
> "Perhaps I meant you to say so, but I meant self-command. You had, somehow or other, broken bounds yesterday, and run away from your own management."

"Self-command" in this novel is a matter of possessing your own tone of voice, of not surrendering it to artificial convivialities or to the styles of social pretension. Even while discussing the matter, however, Emma admits to a flirtatious game with Churchill — "perhaps I intended you to say so" — and to want or need flattery is in itself to be only precariously under "your own management." In the ensuing dialogue she is soon to lose her "own management" to his, as he becomes first in tone and then by explicit admission the master of "ceremonies" in a theatrical entertainment for the benefit of Miss Woodhouse. In what follows, as Emma is rapidly and audibly drawn into the artifices of Frank Churchill, many of them meant to hurt Jane Fairfax, there is a stunning demonstration of how Jane Austen's psychological and historical acuteness is inseparable from her concepts of nature *in* social structures. Churchill's theatricality has the momentary effect of shaping Highbury society into artificial forms which twist and even destroy some of its habitual responsibilities. Emma's remark that the two of them are "talking nonsense for the entertainment of seven silent people," acknowledges the quality of the situation for which he, in reply, is willing to take full credit:

> "I say nothing of which I am ashamed," replied he, with lively impudence. "I saw you first in February. Let everybody on the Hill hear me if they can. Let my accents swell to Mickleham on one side, and Dorking on the other. I saw you first in February." And then whispering — "Our companions are excessively stupid. What shall we do to rouse them? Any nonsense will serve. They *shall* talk. Ladies and gentlemen, I am ordered by Miss Woodhouse (who, wherever she is, presides,) to say, that she desires to know what you are all thinking of."

> Some laughed, and answered good humouredly. Miss Bates said a great deal; Mrs. Elton swelled at the idea of Miss Woodhouse is presiding; Mr. Knightley's answer was the most distinct.

> "Is Miss Woodhouse sure that she would like to hear what we are all thinking of?"

> . . . "It is a sort of thing," cried Mrs. Elton emphatically, "which *I* should not have thought myself privileged to inquire into. Though, perhaps, as the *Chaperon* of the party — *I* never was in any circle — exploring parties — young ladies — married women —"

Her mutterings were chiefly to her husband;
and he murmured in reply,

"Very true, my love, very true. Exactly so,
indeed — quite unheard of — but some ladies
say any thing. Better pass it off as a joke. Every
body knows what is due to *you*."

"It will not do," whispered Frank to Emma,
"they are most of them affronted. I will attack
them with more address. Ladies and gentlemen — I am ordered by Miss Woodhouse to
say, that she waives her right of knowing exactly what you may all be thinking of, and
only requires something very entertaining
from each of you, in a general way. Here are
seven of you, besides myself, (who, she is
pleased to say, am very entertaining already,)
and she only demands from each of you either
one thing very clever, be it prose or verse, original or repeated — or two things moderately
clever — or three things very dull indeed, and
she engages to laugh heartily at them all."

"Oh! very well," exclaimed Miss Bates,
"then I need not be uneasy. 'Three things very
dull indeed.' That will just do for me, you
know. I shall be sure to say three dull things as
soon as ever I open my mouth, shan't I? —
(looking round with the most good-humoured
dependence on every body's assent) — Do not
you all think I shall?"

Emma could not resist.

"Ah! ma'am, but there may be a difficulty.
Pardon me — but you will be limited as to
number — only three at once."

Miss Bates, deceived by the mock ceremony
of her manner, did not immediately catch her
meaning; but, when it burst on her, it could
not anger, though a slight blush showed that it
could pain her.

"Ah! — well — to be sure. Yes, I see what she
means (turning to Mr. Knightley,) and I will
try to hold my tongue. I must make myself
very disagreeable, or she would not have said
such a thing to an old friend."

"I like your plan," cried Mr. Weston.
"Agreed, agreed. I will do my best. I am making a conundrum. How will a conundrum
reckon?"

"Low, I am afraid, sir, very low," answered
his son; — "But we shall be indulgent —
especially to any one who leads the way."

"No, no," said Emma, "it will not reckon
low. A conundrum of Mr. Weston's shall clear
him and his next neighbour. Come, sir, pray
let me hear it."

"I doubt its being very clever myself," said
Mr. Weston. "It is too much a matter of fact,
but here it is. — What two letters of the alpha-
bet are there, that express perfection?"

"What two letters! — express perfection! I
am sure I do not know."

"Ah! you will never guess. You, (to Emma),
I am certain will never guess. — I will tell
you. — M. and A. — Em — ma. — Do you understand?"

Understanding and gratification came together. It might be a very indifferent piece of

wit; but Emma found a great deal to laugh at
and enjoy in it. . . .

When the insult is felt by Miss Bates, she turns confidently only to Knightley. It is missed by the others in
the growing fakery and game-playing of the scene and
obscured, even for its victim, by the degree to which
speech has by now become merely a game of words. The
consciously theatrical declarations of Churchill — "Let
my accents swell to Mickleham" — make Emma the center of a proposed entertainment. The term "entertainment" is repeated twice just before the moment when
Emma, thoroughly swept up and now forgetting her
proper relationship to Miss Bates and to the rest of the
group, cannot resist the opportunity for an "entertaining" retort. She seizes an occasion — one that would
indeed be exploited in a witty play — and the result, to
the hypothetical witness Mark Twain, might easily take
its place within the moral category of Huck's insult to
Jim on the raft, also the consequence of a game apparently no less innocent. If Miss Bates is momentarily deceived by the "mock ceremony" of Emma's manner,
Emma is herself deceived by it for an even longer time.
She is not even aware of what has happened, and enters
immediately into a word game that is no more than a
formal version of what has already been going on. The
game involves the disguise of Emma's name by the play
of Mr. Weston's voice, just as her identity has effectively
been disguised by the role she plays in Frank's entertainment. Again, there is a stressed similarity of father
and son, despite their obvious differences, and it is indicative of Mr. Weston's unresponsiveness to the inner

movements of social life, his capacity to deal only with
its surface, with the games that can hold it together,
that, immmediately after the insult and apparently
oblivious to it, he proposes a further entertainment for
Miss Woodhouse, the "conundrum." Emma is at a point
where her "understanding" is plainly the victim of her
"gratification," but Jane Austen is not anxious, given
the alternatives available to Emma in this society, that
the reader judge her heroine severely. The deflection of
our criticism is brilliantly timed by making us see how
anxious Mrs. Elton is to offer hers. Her "swelling," re-
plete with a touch of French, reminds us of affectations
in Highbury more unpalatable even than Frank's "swelling" speech. She is the more vulgar of the two because
more given wholly to social pretention, much like her
*caro sposo*, as she calls him, who chirps in with his "exactly so," "indeed."

The scene itself "swells" with increasingly "mock
ceremony," a phrase that is weighted with crucial significances from earlier parts of the novel. It is "mock
ceremony" that in fact causes the violation of social
responsibility at Box Hill and disrupts the natural order
of relationships to which Knightley will refer when he
chastises Emma. In contrast is the "unceremoniousness
of perfect amity" illustrated in the scene with Emma,
Knightley and the children, and the earlier description
of Knightley, the hero of Box Hill and the novel, as having "nothing of ceremony about him." His criticisms of
Emma in this scene draw power, therefore, from his
having been given control in the novel of recurrent
phrases and terms like "amiable" that define, in his use
of them, the best form, as Jane Austen herself sees it, of

English society. Indeed, he finally gives "ceremony" its most positive meaning when the term is used at the end to describe his marriage to Emma. And his impatient question to her at Box Hill — "How could you be so un-feeling to Miss Bates?" — carries the general force of his earlier definition of "English delicacy" and suggests that, in lacking it, Emma may be in more than one sense a "denaturalized" citizen. Partly by such recurrences of phrasing, the scene becomes a drama of English natural-ness of manner opposed to "French" mannerism, much as *Huckleberry Finn,* in the scenes on the raft, drama-tizes a conflict between naturalness and the imported literary styles that characterize the expression of every-one in the novel except Jim and sometimes Huck.

The quite unexpected affinities between Jane Austen and Mark Twain — affinities that make the very differ-ent values they give to the same words, like the word "natural," the more revealing — are perhaps summar-ized in the treatment given Mrs. Elton, a fraud and masquerader to a degree Mark Twain would have rel-ished. As an example, she imagines a party at Knight-ley's which will be held out of doors so that it can be as "natural and simple as possible." ("I shall wear a large bonnet, and bring one of my little baskets hanging on my arm . . . a sort of gipsy party.") Knightley's reply, typically direct and restrained, affirms how much for Jane Austen, as for him, words like "simple" and "natu-ral" can be defined very adequately by an uncompli-cated observation of unfussy social habits:

> "Not quite. My idea of the simple and the nat-ural will be to have the table spread in the dining-room. The nature and the simplicity of

gentlemen and ladies, with their servants and furniture, I think is best observed by meals within doors. When you are tired of eating strawberries in the garden, there shall be cold meat in the house."

The dramatic issue of the novel is in a sense whether or not Emma, as she herself fears just before the episode at Box Hill, is to be considered "of Mrs. Elton's party." This, like every phrase in the episode, has a metaphoric resonance drawn from the entire novel. To be "of Mrs. Elton's party" is a metaphor for submitting to social forms in which Mrs. Elton's false, affected, and pretentious ideas of the "natural" predominate, just as similar ideas fully control the society of *Huckleberry Finn.* Indeed, to be thought "natural" by society in Mark Twain's novel means that you must have imitated a prescribed role. The stakes for Jane Austen and her heroine are very high indeed — to prevent society from becoming what it is condemned for being in *Huckleberry Finn.*

## II

Mark Twain cannot imagine a society in which his hero has any choice, if he is to remain in society at all, but to be "of Tom Sawyer's party." The evidence for such a comparative limitation on the hero — and, indeed, a justification for making a comparison to the greater freedom allowed Emma — is in the similarity between the situations of the two characters at the central crisis in each book. Beside the famous picnic scene at Box Hill, when the heroine insults Miss Bates, can be

placed the corresponding scene in *Huckleberry Finn*
when, in Chapter xv, Huck also insults a social inferior
who is at the same time a trusting friend. The process by
which each of these insults comes about is roughly the
same. Emma at Box Hill gradually surrenders what
is called her "self-command" to the theatrical urgings
and flatteries of Frank Churchill, while Huck often acts
in imitation of the "style" of Tom Sawyer even when it
doesn't suit him. Emma literally forgets who she is and
therefore the identity of Miss Bates in relation to her,
and her witty retort to one of the older lady's simplicities expresses not her true relationship to Miss Bates so
much as the theatrical and self-aggrandizing role which
Churchill has encouraged her to play to the whole
group. Her social and psychological situation — and the
literary problem thus created — is much like Huck's at
the similar moment when imitation of Tom's role has
led to his violation of the bond between him and Jim.
The central character in each novel has violated a social
contract by being artificial. Both recognize what has
happened and both make amends. But at this point
there appears an important and essential difference between the situations of these two, and the difference is
indicative of the problem in American nineteenth-
century fiction of imagining personal relationships within the context of existent social environments. Huck's
recognition cannot involve a choice, as can Emma's,
against some forms of social expression in favor of
others: against the Frank Churchills, Mrs. Eltons (and
Tom Sawyers) of this world, and for the Mr. Knightleys.
Mark Twain simply cannot provide Huck with an alternative to "games" that has any viability within the social
organization which the novel provides. Huck's promise

to do Jim "no more mean tricks" is, in effect, a rejection of the only modes of expression understood by his society. At a similar point Emma recognizes and rejects social artifice and is then in a position to accept her natural place in society as Knightley's wife.

Huck chooses at the end "to light out for the Territory ahead of the rest," while Emma, joined to Knightley in "the perfect happiness of the union," is both firmly within a social group and yet saved from all the false kinds of undiscriminating "amiability" practiced at Box Hill. The ceremony is witnessed, significantly, not by the whole community but by a "small band of true friends." "Marriageableness," as Emerson scornfully puts it, emphatically is Jane Austen's subject. Marriage represents for her what he chooses to slight — not merely the act of choice within society but, more importantly, the union of social and natural inclinations. Naturalness and social form are fused in her work in a way that I do not think Emerson, Mark Twain of *Huckleberry Finn*, or even Henry James were able sufficiently to value. It is no wonder that Mark Twain's difficulties begin at a comparable point where Jane Austen most brilliantly succeeds. *Huckleberry Finn* cannot dramatize the meanings accumulated at the moment of social crisis because the crisis itself reveals the inadequacy of the terms by which understandings can be expressed between the hero and other members of his society. There is no publicly accredited vocabulary which allows Huck to reveal his inner self to others.

The comparison between Huck and Emma offers at least a tentative answer to a question of some significance, not merely for *Huckleberry Finn,* but for other American novels of the century in which there is a lim-

ited view of the inclusiveness of social environments
and of the language that holds them together. The
question again is why, precisely at Box Hill, Jane Austen is able to see her way clear to a dramatic resolution
of the meaning of her novel, while Mark Twain is
stalled at a similar point to a degree that makes him observe, in a letter to Howells, that he liked his novel
"only tolerably well, as far as I have got, and may possibly pigeonhole or burn the MS when it is done"? The
threat, only partly in jest, was made in August 1876. In
barely a month almost a third of the novel had been
written. It was not to be finished for seven years. It had
reached a point where Huck, having tricked and then
apologized to Jim, decides that he can no longer exploit
his Negro friend with tricks but will instead try to save
him by tricking society. By his decision not to use the
"style" of Tom on a runaway slave (Chapter xv), Huck
gives up conformist for rebellious trickery. In Chapter
XVI, at the point where the novel came to a halt in 1876,
Huck, halfway between the raft and the shore, intends
to betray his companion. Instead he saves him from cap-
ture by inventing an elaborate lie, persuading the two
men in the skiff that the raft is occupied by the boy's
contagiously sick father. Chapters xv and xvi constitute
what I shall be calling the "reversal scenes": they bring
about the dramatic crisis by which Huck decisively
reverses, for a time, the Tom Sawyerish trend in his relationship to Jim; and they also reverse his efforts to belong imaginatively to society, as most attractively represented by that "respectable" boy Tom Sawyer.

My explanation of Mark Twain's difficulty at this
point and of why, after it, his greatest novel goes to
pieces will not, I hope, suggest that *Huckleberry Finn*

is inferior to *Emma,* whatever that would mean. For one thing, I cannot imagine how *Huckleberry Finn* could have succeeded in resolving the issues that it creates. It makes nothing less than an absolute disavowal, after Huck lies to protect Jim, of any significant dramatic relationship between the hero and all the other characters, whose habitual forms of expression define what I mean by "society" in this novel. The failure is predictable and inescapable in view of the accomplishment, never adequately described by commentaries on the novel, of the first sixteen chapters. These chapters reveal an experimental mastery beyond anything that the author's other works would allow us to expect. Henry Nash Smith points out, perhaps forgetting *The Blithedale Romance,* that not even Henry James had ever dared, by 1885, when *Huckleberry Finn* was published as a book, to entrust the point of view so fully to a character of such evident individuality. My reservations about this judgment are mostly in the interest of pointing to accomplishments and complexities in excess merely of manipulating point of view. For one thing, it cannot be demonstrated that Huck's point of view is maintained with any success throughout the book. The novel is remarkable for the degree to which the hero's voice — from which his point of view is deduced — becomes increasingly inaudible. Even at the beginning, the author uses his narrator to create, all unknown to him and through what are made to seem the most natural habits of his mind — its tendency to verbal repetition — a metaphorical definition of society as no more than a fabrication of art and artifice. Thus, even while we are hearing in Huck's voice a desire for accommodation to this society, as exemplified in Tom, we are seeing in these repeated metaphors Mark Twain's own alienation from that society.

The Shakespearean use of language in the opening chapters allows Mark Twain to blend immediacy and significance, pictorial entertainment and metaphoric implication, in a way that imperceptibly ties the destiny of the narrator to the destiny of the culture defined by Mark Twain's images. In a style that has the easy movement of a boy's story and a compactness usually found only in poetry of considerable density, these early pages reveal a society shaped entirely by fantasy and illusion and that depends for sanction primarily on literary authority. Unlike Emma, who is offered many ways of speaking and may choose even from among competitive definitions of words, Huck's language is rigidly controlled by people who are essentially alien to him. To both adults and companions he sounds like a "numb-skull" because he takes them at their word and finds that he is thereby taken in. By assuming that their statements have at least some literal meaning, he unintentionally discovers the actual self-interest or self-delusion behind their language. These are rather grim suggestions, when in fact the experience of reading the opening chapters is not grim at all and answers the objection, best phrased by Poe, that if allegory "ever established a fact, it is by dint of overturning a fiction." Poe's attack on Hawthorne includes a description of an alternative to allegorical simplicities that might be applied to the metaphoric structure I am about to examine:

> Where the suggested meaning runs through the obvious one in a *very* profound undercur-

rent, so as never to interfere with the upper
one without our volition, so as never to show
itself unless *called* to the surface, there only,
for the proper uses of fictitious narrative, is it
available at all.

The undercurrent has been indeed so "very pro-
found" that it has never been clearly exposed beneath
the surface of the first three chapters, which even some
recent commentators have described as belonging to the
tradition of *Tom Sawyer*. Such a reaction should not too
quickly be dismissed, however. The narrative voice at
the beginning does in fact lull our attention to implications lurking in it. The implications are contemptuous
of the tradition of *Tom Sawyer*, even while the voice is
not nearly so anxious to be separated from it. As early
as the second paragraph there is a metaphoric equation
which effectively condemns society as embodied in Tom
Sawyer; yet the condemnation is so clearly the uninten-
tional revelation of Huck's mind that it is as if Mark
Twain himself is trying to exorcise it. Huck's voice is
like a screen protecting the author from the abstractions
implicit in his own metaphors:

> The Widow Douglas she took me for her son,
> and allowed she would sivilize me; but it was
> rough living in the house all the time, consid-
> ering how dismal regular and decent the
> widow was in all her ways; and so when I
> couldn't stand it no longer, I lit out. I got into
> my old rags, and my sugar-hogshead again, and
> was free and satisfied. But Tom Sawyer, he
> hunted me up and said he was going to start a

> band of robbers, and I might join if I would go
> back to the widow and be respectable. So I
> went back.

Tom Sawyer's games are intimately related, it is implied, to the "respectable" aspects of adult society. The
alternative to both is "freedom," with Huck caught between his impulsive need for it and his equally strong
need for company: "so I went back." It is metaphori-
cally suggested that Tom Sawyer and Widow Douglas
are in tacit alliance, and both are indicted by the further suggestion that to be "respectable" in her terms is
the necessary condition for membership in his gang.
"Respectable" society as represented by the Widow is
equivalent to a "band of robbers." The parallel is then
advanced, with relevance to social artificiality of a specifically literary sort, by the account of Huck's training
with the Widow. Evocations of "her book," her Biblical
authority for believing things that are not true for
Huck, anticipate the even more frequent references in
the next and later chapters to Tom's "books," the romances which are also "authorities" for illusion. Before
this equation is developed, however, Huck turns for the
first time in the novel away from society, not by "lighting out" but by entering into a soliloquy which is in
part a communion with nature and spirits. He turns,
like Emerson at the opening of *Nature,* not only away
from people but also away from "books," from the
"study" which Emerson, in the first paragraph of his
essay, also rejects for the "stars":

> Miss Watson she kept pecking at me, and it got
> tiresome and lone-some. By-and-by they
> fetched the niggers in and had prayers, and

then everybody was off to bed. I went up to my
room with a piece of candle and put it on the
table. Then I set down in a chair by the window and tried to think of something cheerful,
but it warn't no use. I felt so lonesome I most
wished I was dead. The stars were shining, and
the leaves rustled in the woods ever so mourn-
ful; and I heard an owl, away off, who-whooing
about somebody that was dead, and a whip-
powill and a dog crying about somebody that
was going to die; and the wind was trying to
whisper something to me and I couldn't make
out what it was, and so it made the cold shivers
run over me. Then away out in the woods I
heard that kind of a sound that a ghost makes
when it wants to tell about something that's on
its mind and can't make itself understood, and
so can't rest easy in its grave and has to go
about that way everynight grieving. I got so
downhearted and scared I did wish I had some
company.

At the outset the reader might be so beguiled by
Huck's narrative voice as to forget not only the metaphoric implications in his language but also that, except
for his address to the reader, he is remarkably quiet. He
speaks infrequently to anyone else; he is seldom heard
in conversation, and he is always inconspicuous in company, even in the "gang." His loneliness, we might say,
is a want of conversation, a lack, in terms of the literary
problem raised by the book, of dramatic relationships.
He listens for sounds from nature and interprets them
more confidently than language, which tends to confuse

or disturb him. "But I never said so," is one of his characteristic comments. The form of the book itself, an autobiography that is also a kind of interior monologue, testifies to the internalization of his feelings and reactions.

And yet, it is necessary to stress that any Emersonian detachment from society for the companionship of the "stars" would never satisfy Huck (or Mark Twain) for very long. His soliloquies are punctuated with the words "lonesome" and "lonely," ending in the present instance with the direct admission that "I did wish I had some company." Company is announced from below the window in the animal noises of Tom Sawyer, and the first chapter ends with tones of deep companionable satisfaction: "Then I slipped down to the ground and crawled among the trees, and, sure enough, there was Tom Sawyer waiting for me."

The organization of the chapter suggests, with pleasure and excitement, that by joining Tom Huck has escaped social entrapment and achieved a Laurentian kind of "freedom" — "freedom together." But Chapter II, with Tom's incessant talk about rules, gangs, and especially books and authority, only confirms the early hint of an essential solidarity between Tom's world and the Widow's, despite her amused assurance that Tom will not qualify for her heaven. Tom's world is dominated by games and fantasies imitated from literature, just as hers is based on illusions derived from religion and the Bible. His tricks, the first of which is an exploitation of Jim in Chapter II, are justified by the "authorities" of boys' games and, by extension, of religion and social respectability, which sanction Miss Watson's exploitation of Jim at still another level. Tom's question in Chapter II when they are discussing the conduct of a game — "Do you want to go to doing different from what's in the books, and get things all muddled up?" — implies even at this point that an argument with the "authority" of boys' games is a disruption of accredited social procedures.

The alternatives promised in Chapter II by Tom's gang and its games to the "civilized" confinements of Chapter I turn out, then, to be no alternatives at all. Offering confirmation of such a reading, Chapter III puts into direct juxtaposition the activities of religious, conservative, respectable society, as embodied in Widow Douglas and Miss Watson, and the activities of children, based on the authorities of romantic literature as interpreted by Tom Sawyer. We have before us the creation in words of a whole society built on games, tricks, and illusions, and the adult version is only superficially different from the children's. You play the game without asking literal-minded questions, play as if it were "for real," or you're a "numb-skull."

The metaphorical equation of the world of adults and of children indicates the relative eccentricity of Huck. Thus while his treatment of Jim during the reversal scenes is a matter of playing one of Tom's tricks, of "playing the game" in the larger sense, his subsequent apology violates the rules of the game as observed both by children and adults. Implicit here, in the most placidly comic part of the book, is what Huck will most painfully discover later: that to give up "tricking" Jim means more than giving up Tom's games. It means, so closely are they imaginatively connected with adult forms of exploitation, that he must also believe himself damned to social ostracism and to Hell.

These significances are not declared nor are they derived merely from images. They are instead the result very often of the similarity of phrasing applied first to the Widow and Miss Watson and then to Tom. The unobtrusiveness by which a parallel is thus established results from the use of phrases having the sound merely of idiomatic repetitiousness, not uncommon in vernacular literature. For example, in the first half of Chapter III, in which Huck is advised by Miss Watson about the advantages of prayer and the Bible, there is a sequence of phrases applied to religion and its promises ("it warn't so," "spiritual gifts," "I couldn't see no advantage to it") that in slightly varied form are applied in the second half to Tom's games and the romantic books which authorize them ("but only just pretended," "done by enchantment," "I couldn't see no profit in it"). In the first half, Huck's literalness, inseparable from a concern for human profit and loss, makes Miss Watson call him a "fool," just as in the second it leads Tom Sawyer to call him a "numb-skull." The list can be extended by anyone who turns to Chapter III, and the implications are in fact summarized in the final sentence of the chapter by Huck himself: "So then I judged that all that stuff was only just one of Tom Sawyer's lies. I reckoned he believed in the A-rabs and the elephants, but as for me I think different. It had all the marks of a Sunday-school." These concluding remarks make the metaphoric intention of the opening chapters unmistakable. Each side of the comparison is modified by the other. Boys' games as Tom plays them are finally, so the comparisons seem to indicate, as genteel and proper as Miss Watson's religion (he always leaves payment for anything he "steals"), and the social respectability and

religion which she represents are, like Tom's games, remote from the requirements of natural, literal, daily
experience, from a concern for elementary human feelings that are revealed in Huck's "numb-skull" skepticism both about games and religion.

But it is time to remind ourselves again that as we
read we are listening to a voice, not drawing metaphoric
diagrams. The voice makes the reading of the metaphors
and any effort to determine their weight within the
total experience of these chapters extremely difficult.
Even at this early point we are uncomfortably aware of
a gap between Mark Twain's position, his view, expressed through these metaphors, of society merely as
system, and the more socially engaged and eager position of the hero. The gap will ultimately mean that the
novel becomes simpler later on than it is here. After the
reversal scenes, personal drama is not allowed to intrude
into a massive parade of social games and disguises.
The sound of Huck's socially involved voice first wavers,
then nearly disappears, then returns as a sickly version
of what we find in these opening scenes. Here, though, it
is heard distinctly enough to make the metaphors amusing and affectionate, however damaging they become if
one isolates their implications.

The great difficulty for the reader in the opening
chapters is that we feel no confidence in balancing the
implications of style, its tendency to repudiate what is at
the same time being affectionately rendered. It is no
wonder that there are many differences of opinion
about the structure of the book and about whether or
not it expresses an ultimate surrender to the so-called
genteel tradition or a final repudiation of it, and of
Hannibal, the so-called Happy Valley of Mark Twain's

youth. Those critics who respond weakly, or not at all, to the metaphoric implications of the early chapters ignore as a consequence the extent to which Mark Twain has begun even here to isolate the consciousness he values from the society in which it seeks to express itself. Put simply, it is predictable from the outset that the book must elect to give its attention either to the development of the hero or to a review of the environment which forestalls that development. The two cannot be synchronized. This literary difficulty is what plagued the author in the summer of 1876, not any discovered contempt of his own, presumably released only by his trip to the Mississippi in 1882, for the environments of his youth. His criticisms are already evident enough in 1876. On the other hand, those who do stress the evidences of repudiation in the early chapters are apt to miss the complications brought about by the freedom Mark Twain allows to the more loving, socially agreeable expressions of his hero. The latter reading is best represented by Leo Marx, whose criticisms of T. S. Eliot and Lionel Trilling for approving of the later portions of the novel have been much admired. But I think the reading he himself offers in his essay confuses Huck Finn with Mark Twain in the opening chapters, not letting us see how much Huck's voice modifies the social criticism, and it then confuses Mark Twain with Huck in the concluding chapters, missing, it seems to me, the degree to which we can only respond to Huck within what has become by then the author's rigidly bitter and impersonal metaphoric design.

What happens to this novel is what happens to Huck at the hands of his creator. The problem for the author after the crucial scenes in Chapters xv and xvi is that the novel can no longer be the autobiography of Huck Finn. It must instead become a kind of documentation of why the consciousness of the hero cannot be developed in dramatic relations to any element of this society. Kenneth Lynn's version of the problem — that after Chapter xvi Mark Twain discovered he must damn the Happy Valley and was loath to do so — has already been paraphrased and questioned in the preceding paragraph. But his reading of this part of the novel can, with some important modifications, take us close to the difficulties that the novelist himself must have felt at this point in the writing. Mark Twain has written himself into a position where he can no longer sustain a double relationship to the social environment of his novel — on the remote contemptuous critic, on the one hand, and, on the other, of the man with illusions that some closer relationship, such as Huck himself seems to want with Tom, can be maintained.

Were we to read the last sentences of Chapter iii as Mr. Marx suggests — "With this statement which ends the third chapter, Huck parts company with Tom" — there would of course be no such problem as I describe. Without Huck's continued longing for some kind of tie with Tom ("respectable" society at its most palatable), the novel would be a relatively unmodified criticism of society carried out by Huck himself, until the author, so Mr. Marx's argument runs, in his essay and in *The Machine in the Garden,* forces a surrender to society at the conclusion. Some such development does occur but it is blurred by the fact that Huck is cultivating an imaginative association with Tom (and therefore society) all the way from Chapter iii to Chap-

ter xv. He consistently imitates him, and to that extent
is, like the rest of this society, imitating "books" and
"authorities." He repeatedly cites Tom as his own authority for tricks and adventures that are conspicuously
at odds with both his feelings and self-interest. The
attractions of social life for Huck, his persistent wish
that "I had some company," are never wholly satisfied by
the companionship of Jim, which explains why, when
they are separated, Huck can so easily put him out of
mind. Tom is evoked, however, no matter how lengthy
the separation. When he frees himself from Pap, with
elaborate trickery in Chapter vii, Huck "did wish Tom
Sawyer was there; I knowed he would take an interest in
this kind of business, and throw in the fancy touches.
Nobody could spread himself like Tom Sawyer in such a
thing as that." In Chapter xii, his escapade on the
*Walter Scott* is justified to Jim by asking, "Do you
reckon Tom Sawyer would ever go by this thing?" and it
could be inferred at this point that Jim, as a companion
on adventures, is implicitly dismissed by the added
remark that "I wish Tom Sawyer *was* here."

The evocation of Walter Scott as a ruined steamboat,
in the context of the metaphors already discussed here,
is itself an image of a romantic, conservative, and religious society in a state of wreckage. What we infer from
the novel alone is confirmed and extended by Mark
Twain's excessive charge (quoted in *Mark Twain in
Eruption*) that Scott was in "great measure responsible
for the Civil War." It was he who made the South fall in
love with "the jejeune romanticism of an absurd past"
and who created "a reverence for rank and cast, and
pride and pleasure in them." Though expressed in 1882
after his visit to the "New South," the attitudes are ap-

parent enough in the early parts of *Huckleberry Finn,*
and the term used to characterize Scott's romanticism,
"jejeune," has a popular meaning that was dramatized
in 1876 in the adventures of boys acting out the romantic predilections of adults. Huck's imitations of
Tom indicate the degree to which he must become an
artificial man, an imitator of literary models, if he is to
be a part of society at all or be accepted by it as a "real"
boy, like Tom.

As the novel moves to the crisis of insult and apology
in Chapter xv, "imitation" is shown, just as at Box Hill,
to result in the loss of "self-command" and an enslavement to alien forms of expression that distort genuine
feelings. Chapter xiv, "Was Solomon Wise?" is a prepar-
atory and comic version of Chapter xv, "Fooling Poor
Old Jim." In the first, the imitative tendencies of Huck
are developed to a point where, with brilliant comic significance, he has stylistically become Tom Sawyer, while
transferring his own identity as a "numb-skull" to Jim
("I said these things are adventures; but he said he
didn't want no more adventures"), and he tries to win
the argument by citing the Widow ("the Widow told
me all about it"). He thus adopts for his "authorities"
the two figures who together represent aspects of the
artifice which, in this novel, are equivalent to society.
Huck, trying to be Tom, bases his arguments on a faith
in symbolic actions, regardless of the practical consequences, while Jim, like Huck himself in earlier arguments with the real Tom, insists on them: "En what use
is half a chile? I wouldn' give a dern for a million of
um." To which Huck replies, much as Tom does to him,
"Hang it, Jim, you've clean missed the point."

Huck's imitation and assumption of Tom's role at this

point prepares us for the crucial scene about to take
place. In the next chapter, after the separation in the
fog, Huck continues the tricks begun by Tom in Chapter II. He tries to convince Jim that he has merely been
dreaming, that what he believed were naturally stimu-
lated feelings of loss and love were the result rather of
fantasy. When Jim realizes that he is being tricked, he
responds with a speech that evokes all the affectionate
trust that has been evident as the unspoken reality of
their relationship. It is only at this point, not at any
earlier one, that Huck does separate himself from Tom:

> It was fifteen minutes before I could work my-
> self up to go and humble myself to a nigger —
> but I done it, and I warn't ever sorry for it
> afterwards, neither. I didn't do him no more
> mean tricks, and I wouldn't done that one if
> I'd 'a knowed it would make him feel that
> way.

The nature of Huck's regret here makes his later
adoption of Tom's name and his later acceptance of
Tom's leadership in the mock freeing of Jim much
more than a sacrifice of the emotional growth registered
in this passage, much more even than a nearly total collapse of Mark Twain's characterization of the hero.
These later developments show the extent to which
Mark Twain, no less than his hero, has fallen victim to
the world structured by this novel. That the circumstances of Huck's characterization, his environmental
placement, make it impossible to sustain the identity he
momentarily achieves in the reversal scenes is apparently recognized by Mark Twain himself in the chapter
immediately following. The very title of it, "The Rat-

tlesnakeskin Does its Work," again suggests how Huck's tricks on Jim always do have painfully real consequences. In this chapter we find Huck trapped in verbal conventions that prevent the release of his feelings in words. The terminology he has been taught to use and that binds him to Tom Sawyer and the others cannot let him express the nature of his relationship to Jim. He feels the "pinch of conscience," which is to say the "pinch" of training, of system, of education. ("It [conscience] is merely a *thing*," according to an entry in Mark Twain's notebooks, "the creature of *training;* it is whatever one's mother and Bible and comrades and laws and systems of government and habitat and heredities have made it.") In the novel, conscience is the product of the "games" of comrades and of the "authorities" of books, including the Bible. The meanings which these impart to Huck's language are inadequate to his feelings. Having been defined most significantly for the reader in scenes of flight with a runaway slave, Huck is still enslaved himself to the language of Tom's settled world, still inescapably attached to it: "Here was this nigger, which I had as good as helped to run away, coming right out flat-footed and saying he would steal his children — children that belonged to a man I didn't even know; a man that hadn't ever done me no harm."

*Huckleberry Finn* is an instance of what happens to a novel when society, as the author conceives it, provides no opportunity, no language, for the transformation of individual consciousness into social drama. The provision is lacking because Mark Twain cannot imagine a society that offers alternatives to artificiality or that has in it, like Joyce's Dublin, evidences of an official culture that has historical dignity and value. Huck's problem

here represents the crisis in the novel itself. This last
quotation, and Huck's use nearby of "right" for what
Mark Twain has made us see is "wrong," of "wrong" for
"right," involves a recognition by the author, more per-
plexed than any it anticipates in Joyce, of what happens
when the hero of a novel must define his alienations
from society in terms that take their meanings for him,
as much as for anyone, from the very "authorities" he
has come to reject. Joyce's theme by choice is Mark
Twain's dilemma. By 1916 Joyce would be so aware of
the problem as a literary and linguistic one that he
would make his hero veritably an artist of words. Stephen Dedalus is a kind of Pateresque Huck Finn. He
tries vainly to dissociate himself from the sources that
give validation to his language — home, church, country
— and he declares his freedom to "change the laws of
nature" in words that reveal, by their associative connections with earlier experiences, his inescapable obligations to the past.

No wonder Mark Twain could not recognize in the
novels of Jane Austen the existence of a society of
alternatives. The existence of such a society in her work
explains the necessary difference between *Emma* and
*Huckleberry Finn* revealed at the point in each where
the social order is disrupted by an insult. In *Emma,* the
crisis results in a restoration to social intercourse of a
naturalness temporarily lost through artifice; in *Huckleberry Finn* it can lead only to the hero's painful and
confused recognition of what his creator has been showing all along — that what is natural for society is in fact
nothing but artifice, tricks, games, and disguise. When
Huck enters society again in Chapter XVII by going
ashore, it is in disguise as George Jackson and among a

group, the Grangerfords, who are given to extravagant forms of genteel and sentimental literary expression and to the romantic waste of a family feud.

To enter society at all as it exists on the shore, to deal with it without disastrous exposure of the sort of person we know him to be, means that throughout the rest of the book Huck must move about in various disguises, tell lies, play roles even more than he has before. And he will at last become "Tom Sawyer" all over again in Chapter XXXII. Still more important, the Huck Finn shown to us at what is obviously the dramatic crisis of the book is disguised thereafter even from the reader. The style of the book after that carries his voice only sporadically: in some lyrical descriptions of life on the raft, and with significant moral complication only once more — for a moment in Chapter XXXI. The implications are historically important: this novel discovers that the consciousness it values most cannot expand within the environment it provides, that the self cannot come to fuller life through social drama, upon which the vitality of this and of most other novels of the last century at some necessary point depend.

There is evidence that Mark Twain himself came to this realization, that he saw his problem in the literary terms in which I am describing it, and that he recognized that his literary dilemma was historically revelatory. The evidence, in addition to his prolonged difficulties in finishing the novel, derives from what the book expresses after the reversal scenes. It never again, except in bits and pieces, expresses the person whose voice there fully answers for almost the last time to the name "Huck Finn." Thereafter, the chapters can be taken as images of justification for Mark Twain's failure to resolve the meanings accumulated at that point. Through a series of burlesque incidents, in some of which Huck plays no part at all — the Grangerfords (XVII–XVIII), the introduction of the King and the Duke (XIX–XX), the Arkansas episodes (XXI–XIII), the Wilks sequence (XXIV–XXIX), and, finally, the staged version of the "freeing" of Jim (XXXIV–XLII) — through these only tenuously linked incidents Mark Twain pictorializes the literary and social conditions which confront the American novelist writing such a book as this. The general implication is that to be born into the world of Huckleberry Finn is to be born, as Hawthorne earlier remarked of all of us, "into a world of artificial system." Between Huck and reality there is always a curtain of "style" — a term sacred to Tom Sawyer. The dominant social style, as these episodes reveal it, is imported and literary, not only from Scott, but also from *Don Quixote*, Casanova, Benvenuto Cellini, and Shakespeare, all mixed with domestic melodrama, the poetry of gift books, and, as in scenes at the Grangerfords, those "novels of costume" that Emerson said had "filled the heads of the most imitative classes" in America.

Mark Twain's arrangement of the scenes involving the Grangerfords and the King and the Duke are especially relevant to the allegorical implications of these later chapters. Having escaped the family feud, a violent expression of the sentimental romanticism that belongs to the painting and poetry of the Grangerfords, Huck is almost immediately trapped by fake royalty, whose imitations have debased Shakespeare into sentimental twaddle. But for a moment in between we are given the beautiful renewal of the idyll of Jim and Huck, so memorable that, though it runs for barely two pages, it

has for some readers become equivalent to the "raft" itself and led to inaccurate schemes that too sharply separate the "raft" from the "shore," elements of which will
very soon possess the raft and the life on it:

> Soon as it was night, out we shoved; when we
> got her out to about the middle, we let her
> alone, and let her float wherever the current
> wanted her to; then we lit the pipes, and dan-
> gled our legs in the water and talked about all
> kinds of things — we was always naked, day
> and night, whenever the mosquitoes would let
> us — the new clothes Buck's folks made for me
> was too good to be comfortable, and besides I
> didn't go much on clothes, no how.

The appearance of the King and the Duke does not,
as sometimes claimed, bring a new element into the
book. They are merely an outrageous example of the
theatricality so persistent from the beginning. They
come to destroy the natural and spontaneous life that
in this very brief interval of time has released its direction not to current styles but to the current of the river,
not to clothes supplied by others but to personal nakedness. We are not allowed simply to equate the "raft"
with "freedom," except as it reminds us of what is to be
lost when the control of it falls almost at once to the
powers of fakery and theatrical enterprise. Huck and
Jim are made literally the prisoners of these things.
They are in the grip of artifice, and their nakedness will
henceforth give way to traveling in costume.

The stylistic organization of the novel, as we have
been observing it, allows us to see the destiny of the
"raft" in still larger terms. The raft is like America

itself, as viewed regionally here by Mark Twain and more generally elsewhere by Cooper, Emerson, and Whitman, all of whom at various times complained not that America was "artless" or "bare," to recall Henry James's description, but that it had surrendered to imitation and a dependence upon foreign models in social conduct and in literature. It had been transformed almost immediately from a place of "nakedness" and "freedom" into what Whitman claimed in 1870, and John Jay Chapman somewhat later, was a "thoroughly upholstered exterior appearance" in excess even of the Old World.

The "Arkansas Difficulty," in Chapters XXI to XXII, contributes to the novel's developing indictment by suggesting how even forms of violence, melodramatic in their own right, effectively touch the feelings of the community only after they have been further stylized and made into a form of entertainment. When Sherburn kills Boggs, the most conspicuous initial reaction is from the "long, lanky man" who does an imitation for the townspeople of what has only just occurred. As the novel describes it, his rendition is in fact a performance for which he is paid by his fellow citizens, who "got out their bottles and treated him." Only then do they join in the unsuccessful lynching bee, as a kind of afterthought: "Well, by and by," the last sentence of the chapter casually begins, "somebody said Sherburn ought to be lynched." The implication that the society of this novel can only feel things that are expressed in ways belonging not to life but to art is apparent still later in the melodrama of "tears and flapdoodle" during the episodes at the Wilks's in Chapters XXIV to XXIX. Here again, the governing style of the community, despite some efforts at good sense, is one of costume drama in which two of the principals are, significantly, pretending to have arrived recently from England. " '*Here* is my answer,' " says Mary Jane when asked to put her English "relatives" to the test: "She hove up the bag of money and put it in the king's hands, and says, 'Take this six thousand dollars, and invest it for me and my sisters any way you want to, and don't give us no receipt for it.' " We are permitted to think, in summary, that the "fine looking man," the social leader who jumps up at the performance of the Royal Nonesuch and admits that "we are sold," is substantially describing the formative processes of society as a whole: the audience should promote the fraudulent theatricals around town, he advises, so that "Then we'll all be in the same boat."

During these episodes, from Chapter xviii to xxix, the freeing of Jim is obviously not the subject of the novel. These chapters are indicative of the fact that the book is concerned with Negro slavery only as one aspect of a more general enslavement — of feeling and intelligence within inadequate and restrictively artificial modes of expression. Dramatically, the book is victim of the conditions illustrated in these chapters, during which Huck is allowed only an attenuated contact with what is going on. His oppositions provide no meaningful dramatic interest. He does not like what is happening — that about sums it up. We witness an intensification of social criticism carried out by episodic illustration and a further development of the metaphors of artifice, but there is no corresponding intensification of drama within the social life that involves Huck. He does help Mary Jane and he does not laugh at the circus performer who he thinks is endangered by the horses, again revealing his lovable seriousness about the human consequences of tricks. But such incidents are themselves flatly representative of relatively static attitudes; they catch none of the complications of response that have been developing up to the reversal scenes. Neither does the remark, by this point tiresomely indicative of a trapped mind slowing down, that "I do believe he [Jim] cared just as much for his people as white folks does for their'n. It don't seem natural but I reckon it's so."

More is lost in that sentence, especially feeble in contrast to Jim's heartbreaking story about his deaf daughter, than the vivid eccentricity of voice that was an earlier indication of Huck's personal, self-critical involvement with life around him. There is a loss even of the vitality of reaction that led to the crucial insult and apology, much less the consequent knowledge of what is "natural" for Negroes. The deterioration is made even more apparent by the degree of explicitness with which Huck is allowed at a few points to condemn the activities he witnesses: "It was enough to make a body ashamed of the human race" is a statement with none of the rewarding complications that have been characteristic of Huck's responses to meanness and his expression of them. Even the vividness of description that results from his spontaneous feelings of relationship to sights and sounds is rarely found in the last half or more of the novel. "If I trod on a stick and broke it, it made me feel like a person had cut one of my breaths in two and I only got half, and the short half, too" — we need only remember such a line as this to recognize how much of Huck has disappeared from the novel when we get to the Arkansas episode and hear what purports to be Huck's description of a town:

On the river front some of the houses was
sticking out over the bank, and they was
bowed and bent, and about ready to tumble
in. The people had moved out of them. The
bank was caved away under one corner of some
others, and that corner was hanging over. People lived in them yet, but it was dangersome,
because sometimes a strip of land as wide as a
house caves in at a time. Sometimes a belt of
land a quarter of a mile deep will start in and
cave along and cave along till it all caves into
the river in one summer. Such a town as that
has to be always moving back, and back, and
back, because the river is always gnawing at it.

Huck is barely present in the language here, the
virtues of which do not include the sound of the identifying narrative voice heard earlier. "People lived in them
yet," or "such a town as that," belong to the narrator of
*Life on the Mississippi,* to Mark Twain himself. It is not
surprising that having put the manuscript of the novel
aside in 1876, near the end of Chapter XVI, he could feel
free to borrow a section of that chapter for *Life on the
Mississippi* in 1882, the famous "raftsmen passage."
And it is of course not irrelevant to my argument
that the borrowing should have come from precisely
the spot where Mark Twain began to feel the difficulty
of maintaining Huck as the dramatic center and narrative voice of his novel.

After the reversal scenes, the novel does not again, for
any considerable stretch, sound like the "autobiography" of Huckleberry Finn until "You Can't Pray a
Lie," Chapter XXXI. There, the language once more ex-

presses some of the musing, characteristically painful effort of Huck to liberate and reveal his complicated feelings. Significantly, there is also a resurgence of the lyricism of description which gives evidence of his affectionate liveliness of response to people and scenery: "and I see Jim before me, all the time, in the day and in the night-time, sometimes moonlight, sometimes storms, and we a-floating along, talking, and singing, and laughing." It seems as if the book is at last re-assembling the hero in a style and situation that will reveal again how dangerously unique he is.

But even here there is a conspicuous repetitiousness, a failure to advance the novel dramatically beyond Chapter XVI. Chapter XXXI is in many ways only a redoing of the earlier crisis, with a "pinch of conscience," a decision, not more or less intense, to do "wrong" and help Jim to freedom. And immediately thereafter, Huck disappears again into the artifices of society. He assumes the identity of Tom Sawyer in Chapter XXXII, "I Have a New Name," and he does so in a phrase ("I was so glad to find out who I was") that pointedly and it seems to me intentionally reminds us of how the movement of the book in its best and most "autobiographical" parts was committed to exactly the opposite development: of Huck's freedom from the imitative artificiality of Tom Sawyer. On the subject of "authorities" and "tricks" by which Tom would "free" the already free Jim, the narrative voice hereafter becomes sickly and accommodating, when it is not timidly pouting: "I ain't going to make no complaint. Any way that suits you suits me." Such a blatant, even contemptuous denial of any dramatic development for which the novel has prepared us, such an articulated destruction of the growth of the hero, seems to me a pathetic admission to the reader of the only grounds on which Huck and his society can be brought into a dramatic relationship that will allow the book to end. Huck's illusion — that Tom has now, shockingly, become revolutionary in his use of tricks — does not modify for the reader the inherently distasteful "literary" quality of Tom's procedures. They would reveal a self-indulgent lack of feeling for the effect of tricks on Jim even if they were intended actually to free him.

It is necessary to repeat that this development cannot in any sense represent a surrender by Mark Twain to the genteel tradition. The split implicit in the opening chapters between Huck's narrative and the author's surreptitious metaphorical ordering of it has now become a chasm between worlds. From the remoteness of a confused repudiation, Mark Twain witnesses with as much exasperation as we do the evidence that to remain in the society of the novel at all requires the capitulation that Huck has made to Tom. The author's judgment of Tom at the end is implied in a number of ways that belong to the impersonal metaphoric structure he has created, even while dramatically the novel can only show Huck in his acts of sulking agreement. The metaphoric pattern implies an important degree of similarity between Tom, and the King and the Duke. His tricks, like theirs, are designed to exploit human feeling, while their own feelings are called forth only by artificial stimulation. The King and the Duke can slobber over Shakespeare and their own fabricated melodrama, knowing that their audience will do the same, and Tom can make up epitaphs for Jim ("here a captive heart busted") and be so carried away by his own versions of phrases scrawled

on prison walls by such heroes as the Count of Monte
Cristo that his "voice trembled, whilst he was reading
them, and he most broke down." The three are related
even more specifically, however, in their treatment of
Jim. In a book so given to parallels, much is implied by
the fact that at the end Tom gives Jim forty dollars for
playing games with his freedom and that this is precisely
the sum paid the King for selling Jim as a runaway.
While the parallel is not exact, it is sufficiently indicative of the value to either party of Jim's remaining in
bondage, even if in Tom's case the prolonging of his enslavement is in the interest not of economics but of
games and adventures.

The style and design of any book trains us as we read
to respond in some ways and not others to certain uses of
language, to find some kinds of conversation artificial
and others natural. It matters very little, therefore, that
in some other book the author approves of certain kinds
of behavior if in the one we are reading he has managed
to make them ambiguously attractive or even reprehen-
sible. *Huckleberry Finn* so insistently educates us to
feelings of exasperation about tricks, games, and theatricality that we cannot have learned our lessons and want
when we reach the last chapters still to be entertained
by Tom's prolonged antics. The uncertainty that one
feels, nevertheless, about the intended effect of the concluding scenes results from the fact that the weight of
prejudice urged upon us by what precedes so brutally
outbalances Tom's innocuous behavior.

Mark Twain's metaphoric rejection of society in this
book saps the potential energy of any of the dramatic
relationships within it. The effect is apparent in his
lassitude and indifference at the end when he shows

Huck Finn confronted by the representative members
of this society, young or old. Mark Twain's distaste for
Tom and Aunt Polly in their final conversation is directed at their characteristically seeing even one another
as embodiments of style and as acting out stereotyped
roles. What Aunt Polly really wants in Tom is a literary
"good-bad boy," so long as his actions are "bad" only as
a "good" boy's should be:

> "Then what on earth did *you* want to set
> him free for, seeing he was already free?"
> "Well, that is a question, I must say; and
> *just* like women! Why, I wanted the *adven-
> ture* of it; and I'd 'a'waded neck-deep in blood
> to — goodness alive, *Aunt Polly!*"
> If she warn't standing right there, just inside
> the door, looking as sweet and contented as an
> angel half-full of pie, I wish I may never!

The cloying effect of this passage is obvious. And yet
the reaction of the reader to it is strangely muffled by
Huck's presentation. It is apparent that he does not respond in the way the book has prepared the reader to
respond, and that he is here glaringly unlike the character we have loved and respected earlier in the book.
What is most significant, however, is that Mark Twain
does not seem to think it matters much that Huck be
given any place in the scene at all. His unctuous "angel
half-full of pie" and the effeminate exclamation "I wish
I may never!" merely scan the scene in terms too abundantly provided by it already. He is merely *of* the scene,
uncritically absorbed into it.

Huck is given back to us at the very end in his decla-
ration of independence, but it is significant that he is

re-created primarily in the image of flight, of "lighting out for the Territory ahead of the rest." He is a character who can exist at all only outside the society that the novel allows us to imagine, who can exist in our imagination, finally, only outside the novel itself. Understandably, Huckleberry Finn became for Mark Twain a kind of obsession, appearing in the years that followed in various sketches for stories and sequels to the novel. It is as if his creator wanted yet another chance to find a home, to build a world, to make a place for him. And yet each version only further disfigures the wondrous boy created in the first sixteen chapters of *Huckleberry Finn*.

The career of this character reveals a great deal about the career of Mark Twain and of American literature just before the turn of the century. As Huck Finn gradually disappears from the novel, Mark Twain himself becomes absorbed in social panorama. Santayana's familiar comment about American humorists helps us understand only the preliminary stages of the process: they "only half escape the genteel tradition," he writes, and they cannot abandon it because "they have nothing to put in its place." What interests me in this, as in other instances of uncompleted rebellion in American writing, are the initial struggles in language, struggles which provide in *Huckleberry Finn*, as in other works we've considered, most of their exotic and unforgettable life. And what is still more interesting is that once Mark Twain gives up the struggle to bring Huck to verbal consciousness within his social environment, once he surrenders Huck's consciousness to that environment, he then shows a zestful appetite for environmental delineation. It does not matter that he increasingly came to see the world as the "mysterious stranger" was to see it — as only "the silly creations of an imagination that is not conscious of its freaks." From a literary point of view it is important only that as this attitude took hold of him he became fascinated in the detailed lineaments of what he claimed to find oppressive. In this he predicts and helps define the essential quality of an emerging naturalistic strain in American fiction. His distaste for Jane Austen is an example of the theoretical quality of his distaste for "society"; he was incapable of knowing what the concept could have meant to her. Nonetheless, and despite the condemnation of authorized environments in *Huckleberry Finn,* the novel lavishes energy and attention on the artificial worlds of force, on a spectacular review of them. Huck Finn and his introverted voice are sacrificed to social panorama, the dominant aspect of the last half of the novel and the determining mode of the two novels with which this present study concludes: *Sister Carrie,* published only fifteen years later, and *The House of Mirth.*

# V

## Panoramic Environment
## and the Anonymity of the Self

Before his close friendship with Edith Wharton, and before he knew very much about her work, James wrote to Howells about the comic proposition that she "belonged" in New York more than he or his works ever could. Talking about his own writings and about hers, he characteristically speaks of fiction as a house among houses, as the building made within already constructed ones. He was responding to Howells's news that an apartment house had been opened in New York City named the *Henry James:*

> Your most kind communication . . . in respect to the miraculously-named "uptown" apartment house has at once deeply agitated me and wildly uplifted me. The agitation as I call it, is verily but the tremor, the intensity of hope, of the delirious dream that such a stroke may "bring my books before the public," or do something toward it — coupled with the reassertion of my constant, too constant conviction that no power on earth can ever do that. . . .

> The *Henry James*, I opine, will be a terrifically
> "private" hotel, and will languish like the Lord
> of Burleigh's wife under the burden of an hon-
> our "unto which it was not born." Refined,
> liveried, "two-toileted," it will have been a
> short lived, hectic paradox, and will presently
> have to close in order to reopen as the Mary
> Johnston or the Kate Douglas Wiggin or the
> James Lane Allen. Best of all as the Edith
> Wharton.

Ostensibly, James is simply being wry about the relative
unpopularity of his later books compared to Mary John-
ston's *To Have and To Hold* or to Mrs. Wiggin's children's books, the most famous of which, *Rebecca of
Sunnybrook Farm,* was to appear the next year, or to
James Allen's *The Choir Invisible*. And although he
was only beginning to take Edith Wharton seriously — a
few months later he was to read the just published and
very un-Jamesian novel *The Valley of Decision* — James
knew when he wrote to Howells in 1902 that she was
then more of a public success for her stories than was he
for his recent popular failure *The Wings of the Dove*.

But the letter is not merely about popularity. It is
also about "building," and it is written by a man who
was always talking about the *house* of fiction. He is simply astonished here that his house could conceivably fit
into the environment of New York. As he imagines the
building, it creates within itself an atmosphere altogether alien to anything outside it: refined, liveried, two-
toileted. What houses of fiction do fit into the environment of New York, of America? James is implying that
in novels more popular than his the created envi-

ronments in no way challenge the authenticity of what people of New York or elsewhere ordinarily take their environment to be. The subservience of such books to the popular consensus is evident in ways only seemingly contradictory: some pretend to offer intensified versions of life as it is commonly lived, while others are ostentatiously artificial in the manner of historical romances. In the one case there is a compliance with reality simply in the effort faithfully to mirror it, in the other there is the emphatic admission that it is impossible even to create the *illusion* of an alternative reality. Historical romances and children's books may give the reader a glimpse of mysterious, fantastic worlds, but never with the striving nobility of intention that Santayana, echoing Emerson and predicting Stevens, ascribed to poetry: "To make us citizens, by anticipation, in the world we crave." The word "anticipation" eloquently implies that our craving is for something that has never yet come into existence, that has presently no form outside the imagination, and can therefore be the effect only of the "poetry" itself.

Therein lies the difference between Edith Wharton and Henry James — in his greater ambition, his confidence in the power of language to make us citizens in the world we crave, rather than in the world where we actually live. It is the difference, too, between the two lines in American literature which, with much crisscrossing, these two writers can be said to represent. That James and Mrs. Wharton resembled one another in important ways has been a stubborn and, except possibly in Mrs. Wharton's *The Reef,* erroneous assumption, despite what Irving Howe and others have argued to the contrary. It took a recent, very able book, Millicent

Bell's *Edith Wharton and Henry James: The Story of Their Friendship,* to make the necessary discriminations. In what each chose to "do" with often similar novelistic circumstances, the two are quite markedly different. Mrs. Wharton herself offered the term "chronicle-novel" to describe her customary manner of doing things, and acknowledged, for contrast, that James "cared only for the elaborate working out on all sides of a central situation." Part of Mrs. Wharton's satisfaction with the simple and sequential ordering of events reflects the fact that her characters are propelled mostly by environmental circumstances external to them. These circumstances were for her not subject to fragmentation or redirection by the exertion of individual needs. There is nothing similarly naturalistic in James, who in eschewing for the most part the conventions of the "chronicle-novel" tried to let the ingredients of events actually reside in the consciousness of his characters. That consciousness often *is* the environment in which his characters contend with their fate. James's grotesquely inclusive later style was designed so that his favorites might indulge in the images and verbal exaggerations necessary to their illusion of freedom, their dream that they create the world they live in. By contrast, the clarity, even to crispness, of Mrs. Wharton's writing indicates a world palpably there in some imposing organization antecedent to anyone's wishes.

But however different from James at his most characteristic, Edith Wharton is heir to the perplexities he confronted and which confused Mark Twain in *Huckleberry Finn.* In so representative a work as *The House of Mirth,* society offers no mode of action, no expression beyond mimicry or silence by which Lily Bart can re-

veal the best impulses in her nature. Like Mark Twain,
Mrs. Wharton succeeds only sporadically in imagining
circumstances in which such revelations can easily take
place; in both writers, favorable environments are associated with an elusive myth of "natural" life, eco-
nomically impoverished but emotionally rich, utterly
marginal, but, within itself, full of close, familial attachments. Similar difficulties with novelistic environment provide a sort of justification for James's later
fiction; they suggest why he chose to create through
his style some more hospitable world for not dissimilar
heroic figures. His heroes are different from theirs, however, in being aware, self-consciously and initially, that
they are risking their freedom of consciousness by efforts
to express it through social manners. Theirs is "the
tragedy of manners," as Frederick Crews has titled it.

The intriguing quality in Mrs. Wharton and in Dreiser is a phenomenon already noticed in *Huckleberry
Finn:* the fascination, apparent in an intensive, detailed rendering, with the environmental forces that destroy what the authors love. They surrender their interest — literally the space they have in their books — to
the power which forbids individual fulfillment, so that
even sex becomes an aspect of that power rather than an
evidence of private involvement or personal society.
Edith Wharton and Dreiser will always remain compelling because, anticipating Fitzgerald and still later American novelists, they tacitly admit bedazzlement with the
very horrors of the modern scene which obliterate their
even more bedazzled heroes. Of course they wrote in
"protest," but we read them not for that but because
they are more instinctively interested in the panorama
that roused in them the energy of protest.

Not even a novelist so consciously protective of his characters' freedom as James could fail to give enormous weight to environmental forces antagonistic to it. The weight is proportionately heavier in Dreiser, Edith Wharton, and Fitzgerald, however, because their heroes are often anxious to surrender themselves to the powers that destroy them. The vision of the Self joining the formative processes of Nature, of the Self believing it can contend for dominance with the forces of Nature, of the Self believing merely that it can define what it is — these notions give way, as literary situations, to an essentially twentieth-century vision of the Self enthralled (and destroyed) by the power and wealth of the City. Norman Mailer's sado-masochistic provocation of the demons of Power is the latest and most self-conscious expression of this phenomenon.

Most American novelists of the late nineteenth and early twentieth centuries *seem* to be saying that environmental forces have so diminished our concept of the self that any latter day projection of it is necessarily a debasement of the possibilities defined by Cooper, Emerson, Whitman, and Mark Twain. But as I've already suggested, this rationalization cannot hide the fact, conspicuous in the proportions and energy of their attention, that these later writers are less interested in worlds defined by the interaction among persons than in a world invulnerable to them. Like Mark Twain in the last two-thirds of *Huckleberry Finn,* their vision often moves panoramically across the massed phenomena of social and economic structures, and it is only within these that they can see the hero at all.

In a curious way, however, this development still carries an Emersonian variation; Emerson is nearly always a hovering presence in American writing, even in the works of Howells, Edith Wharton, and Dreiser. Once the heroes in their novels discover that they are diminished rather than enlarged by efforts to participate in the massed power around them, they also find that they belong to a mysterious brotherhood of souls, a sort of Over-Soul of the lowly in which personal identities are lost and where all share a common destiny. Dreiser's essay "The Myth of Individuality" might be said to adapt Emerson's idea of the Over-Soul to the metropolis, and his admiration for Emerson was implicit much earlier, even in *Sister Carrie*. Fellow feeling of this sort in the face of the impersonality of urban life gets a polite expression, too, in Howells's idea of "complicity," in Mrs. Wharton's idealization, in some of her works, of the sympathetic companionship of the poor and lowly, and in the powerful desire of Faulkner's Isaac McCaslin for "the communal anonymity of brotherhood," providing as it does a source for the political affirmations in *Intruder in the Dust*. The differences among these writers scarcely needs to be mentioned, but they have in common a vision of modern or city "environment" as offering almost no inducement to the human vanity of controlling, much less building, the world one lives in. Howells manages, of course, to suggest a kind of amelioration: the passage of time, as we see in his charming and ignored *Indian Summer*, simply brings into our daily lives a series of helpful distractions from insoluble situations, until by this very process the situations are bypassed.

Again, *Huckleberry Finn* — though Mark Twain is anticipated in this by the Melville of "Bartleby" and *Pierre* — strikes a note that in a few years becomes a momentarily dominant one in American literature: environment becomes force, totally shaping personal relations while remaining unaffected by them. Personal relations come to be little more than inarticulate human huddles, figurations of basic human needs for warmth and tenderness, for food and shelter. "Panoramic environment and the anonymity of the self" is only the most useful titular summary I can give to this aspect of American literature, and many qualifications to it will need to be made by illustrations from *The House of Mirth* and *Sister Carrie.*

## II

Mrs. Wharton's life was itself a drama of impulse, impulse that apparently never broke through her personal disciplines or her subscription to public ones. The story of her marriage to an increasingly neurasthenic husband, whom she divorced in 1913, and of the emergence earlier, in 1908 when she was 46, of a passion for Walter Berry, an American lawyer in Paris whom she had known since a year before her marriage, is powerfully told by Mrs. Bell, and her most familiar work, *Ethan Frome,* is a melodrama of the frustrations of love trapped within social and seemingly natural orders. Just as surely as she was a woman with unusual power of personality, she used it to restrain rather than to exercise her feelings. She created a visible image of her personality in the organization of her household. At age eleven she wrote a story on the first page of which was the sentence " 'If only I had known you were going to call, I should have tidied up the drawing-room,' said Mrs. Tompkins." To which young Edith's mother re-

sponded with the obviously effective criticism that
"Drawing-rooms are always tidy."

Edith Wharton's drawing rooms always were, as her
friends ruefully observed, whether in her house in
Lenox, Massachusetts, her various apartments in the
Rue de Varenne in Paris, or her houses elsewhere in
France. Her response to France, even to its landscape,
characteristically involved admiration for preordained
order and the discipline of impulse: "Every field has a
name, a history, a distinct place of its own in the village
polity; every blade of grass is there by an old feudal
right which has long since dispossessed the worthless and
original weed." In France, where she lived for thirty
years until her death in Paris in 1937, Mrs. Wharton
found the comforting evidence that there existed historical support for the kind of aristocratic life that had
all but disappeared, according to *A Backward Glance*,
from the New York of her childhood. Daughter of one
of the distinguished families of New York City, where
she was born in 1862, a descendant of Rhinelanders and
Gallatins, she could remark of her fellow expatriot
Henry James that "he belonged irrevocably to the old
America out of which I also came." Few American writers illustrate more eloquently than she the need in life
as well as in novels for some institutional support of
feelings otherwise crushed by institutions. The literary
consequences of her confused feelings about impulse
and order are apparent in the very best of her novels.

*The House of Mirth* was the last of her books written
while New York was still her home, and it is a portrayal
of life in that city during the closing years of the nineteenth century. Her social background might explain
why the book is so mercilessly critical of the commercial

forces that had come to dominate the society of New York, but the novel is equally important as literary biography. She tells us that with the writing of *The House of Mirth* she "was turned from the drifting amateur into a professional." Importantly, her ideals of literary professionalism located themselves less in American than in English literature, and in the great European novelists, Balzac, Turgenev, and Flaubert. While she could say that James was "almost the only novelist who has formulated his ideas about his art," and while her achievements as a satirist prepared the way for Sinclair Lewis, who dedicated *Babbitt* to her, the most prevalent influences in her work came from English novelists of manners.

She turned to English novelists for the support of attitudes no longer articulated within the American society she depicts. The result is a precarious mixture of tones, an evidence of discrepancy between the subject of her satire, which is uniquely American and contemporary, and her dependence at certain points on English writers, especially Jane Austen and George Eliot, who never, even in extremity, felt that their values went unrepresented among the dominant forces in the world around them. As a consequence, neither of them used other writers in the way Mrs. Wharton does — as if literature might provide her with the institutional sanctions she could not receive from her own society. In this Mrs. Wharton reveals an American seriousness about literature as an institution that is the foundation for the literary allusiveness so characteristic of American literature from Hawthorne and Melville to T. S. Eliot.

It is of some historical importance that we can hear

the accents of Jane Austen and the rhetoric of George Eliot in the pages of this novel. Wherever the wit is most secure, wherever it is least strident and least in anticipation of the satirical style of Sinclair Lewis, it is apt to remind us of Jane Austen. Thus when Miss Stepney brings accusations against the heroine to Miss Bart's guardian, there are recognizably literary encouragements from Jane Austen in the remark that Miss Stepney "was not sufficiently familiar with the classic drama to have recalled in advance how bearers of bad tidings are proverbially received, but she now had a rapid vision of forfeited dinners and reduced wardrobe as a possible consequence of her disinterestedness. To the honor of her sex, however, hatred of Lily prevailed over more personal considerations."

In saying that Mrs. Wharton leaned at such points on an earlier English novelist, I don't mean to suggest that Miss Austen herself felt no corresponding dissatisfactions with her own social and historical environment. The very existence of her novels testifies that she did. If Mrs. Wharton felt, as one of her old friends expressed it, that life in America "unconsciously for all of us began to change from simplicity to vulgarity in the late 'eighties," Jane Austen in the first decade of the same century wrote partly in response to a similar process in England. "It is hard indeed," as Armour Craig points out, "not to use the inevitable 'age of transition' in reflecting on the kind of world" Jane Austen presents, a world where it is becoming difficult "even to provide a homogeneous guest list for a ball." But the forces of disruptive change had to make their way through a texture altogether more resilient and more absorbent, less easily discolored than Mrs. Wharton's.

Jane Austen's was a society at once stronger and more flexible than anything that New York, even at its most appealing, could allow Edith Wharton to imagine. Well before the appearance of *The House of Mirth* in 1905, the old conservative families had been replaced by the new ones enriched through the expansion of business. Lily Bart's career takes her through the various strata of society, from top to bottom, and the tracing of her career is coexistent with Mrs. Wharton's panoramic view of the world that bears down on her. She moves from the Trenors of "Bellomont," who feel some of the restraints of "old habits," to the Dorsets, who exploit traditional mores as a disguise for the misconduct eventually paid for by Lily; from the ferociously social-climbing Brys to the uncritically pleasure-seeking Gormers, and from there to the outskirts of social acceptability when Lily becomes a secretary to the latest invader from the Western states, Miss Hatch of the Hotel Emporium. Mrs. Wharton's description of Lily's stay with Miss Hatch includes one of the most incisive pictures in our literature of hotel life in America, reminding us that her preoccupation with environment was evident, too, in her first book of prose — *A Study of Interior Decorating*. Though these various elements struggle for power, their essential qualities blend so easily into one another that there is in this novel actually no dramatized conflict of class or of social values. There are only conflicts of economic and social power, in which the outcome is largely determined by money. Even the efforts of sexual conquest in the book have money as their primary inducement.

One of Mrs. Wharton's subtly achieved implications

is that emotions in this society are calculated and invested with the coldness of financial speculation. For
anyone as financially impoverished as Lily, the alternative to calculation is social ruin. "It was seldom," Mrs.
Wharton reports in a metaphor that unites financial
with emotional economies, that Lily "could allow herself the luxury of an impulse." She is therefore not
being luxurious when we see her in Chapter 2 on a
train — one of her frequent trips to the great country
houses to which her charm, beauty, and little services
win her invitations — "studying her prey through down-
cast lashes while she organized her method of attack."
Her prey is Percy Gryce, limited in all things except
prudery, a collection of Americana, and the millions
which Lily needs if she is to secure a place in the New
York society where her parents went bankrupt maintaining even a foothold. As Mrs. Wharton's style would
suggest, Lily can be taken here as only a comic threat to
poor Percy, and we have just been shown in the opening
chapter that she is really not studious enough to be a
seductress in so theatrical a vein. She has already acted
with the generous impulsiveness that will make her the
"prey" of her proposed victims. While waiting for the
train, she has met Selden, the one man in the book she
truly admires despite his lack of prosperity, and, having
accepted an invitation to his rooms for tea, is discovered
on leaving by Rosedale, a social-climbing Jewish in-
vestor. He is also a gossip, and he promptly catches her in
unnecessary and obvious lies about her reasons for being
in the building.

Lily's mistake and its consequences justify Mrs.
Wharton's claim that in her works "My last page is always latent in my first" — such is the undeflectable force

of the social process. At the end of the novel, Lily's
hope of becoming active again within society rests
with Rosedale, the man who first suspects her deviations
from the rules. Having failed with Gryce out of her
impulsively expressed wishes to be with Selden; having
thoughtlessly accepted what seemed merely the business
advice of Gus Trenor, the husband of her best friend,
only to discover herself compromised by him; having
slipped then to companionship with the Dorsets, where
her kindness to the husband is exploited by the wife as
a cover for her own amatory adventures, Lily is faced
with Rosedale's proposal. He will marry her and give her
financial power over her enemies if she will use some
letters to Mrs. Dorset that have come into her possession
as a way of forcing Mrs. Dorset to withdraw the lies she
has been spreading about her. Lily's failure to carry out
this blackmail is a matter less of ethics than, once again,
of her responding to impulses rather than following the
calculated movements that are consonant with the
rhythms of her environment. On the way to Mrs. Dorset's she happens past Selden's apartment building and
makes, by the sudden decision to visit him, a final grasp
for the life of moral refinement which she sees in him
and which, by her proposed maneuver, she is about to
lose forever for herself. While there, again on an impulse of generous and exalted feeling, she contrives
secretly to burn the letters with which she would have
implicated Mrs. Dorset and Selden. She seals thereby
her social obliteration.

"Obliteration" is not too strong a word to describe
how, near the end of the novel, Lily disappears into the
mass of New York, again panoramically rendered, into
"the thousands of insignificant figures" who watch with

her the parade of fashion, in which she herself once took part, along Fifth Avenue. This is the price exacted for those tiny acts of independence, those generous and sympathetic promptings which have set her apart from society in this book even when she is most assiduously trying to join it. To us as to Selden, her attractiveness is "the way in which she detached herself, by a thousand indefinable shades, from the persons who most abounded in her own style." The analogy to Fitzgerald's Gatsby is obvious enough.

Lily's alertness to the possibilities of life is what defeats her by making her deviate from any settled campaign of success. Though she is unfortunately a spendthrift with money, the society of Trenor and Dorset takes its toll of her because she is admirably a spendthrift of emotions. It is thus characteristic that to her drab little friend Gerty she should give the liberal fraction of the money she is about to spend on a dressing case, and that in her treatment of servants she acts like one "long enough in bondage to other people's pleasures to be considerate of those who depend on hers." In Mrs. Wharton's noble phrase, Lily is capable of "those shocks of pity that sometimes decentralize a life." Indeed, in the environment of this book "eccentricity" describes the few natural rather than the many grotesque characters we encounter, much as it defines Melville's Bartleby who, at the very "center" of American financial power, is treated as an intolerable "eccentric" even while his fellow scriveners, Turkey, Nippers, and Ginger Nut are accepted in their Dickensian grotesqueness as merely amusing and convenient fellows to have around Wall Street.

And yet while Mrs. Wharton is a remarkably tough-minded writer, *The House of Mirth* insists on a rather too easy connection between Lily's freedom of impulse and the fact that she is poor and responsive to the poverty of others. The primitivistic assumption that the life of impulse is somehow located in the lower region of society is common enough in literature and notably so in American writers as otherwise different as Dreiser and Faulkner. In Mrs. Wharton's case, the assumption, once recognized as operative in her book, seems a logical consequence of her very rigid satirical view of the high society wherein Lily's career is initially dramatized. In none of the inhabitants of this society, not even in Selden, who likes to be aloof from it, can Mrs. Wharton locate a sustained expression of uncalculated feeling, anything that might create a countermovement to the system of emotional and financial calculation on which the society is built. Lily's financial precariousness lets her see a reflection of her possible destiny in the lives of the poor as well as the rich, and to see it with an intimidated sympathy. One can sense this sympathetic quality in Lily even in the poignant scenes that reveal her incapacity to love Gerty, the person who helps her most unselfishly. Lily recognizes in Gerty's "acquiescence in dinginess" a terrifyingly close approximation of her own situation, were she without the spirit which makes her so attractively full of hope. Gerty has a "moral vision which makes all human suffering so near and insistent that the other aspects of life fade into remoteness."

Even while Mrs. Wharton is perhaps too glib in the connections she makes between lowliness and human warmth, neither she nor her heroine willingly gives up her appetite for the more glamorous possibilities of life. Poverty felt as a threat, no matter what it offers by way of communal feeling, gives to Mrs. Wharton's descriptions of working-class life and the drabness of Lily's surroundings an immediacy comparable to Dreiser's *Sister Carrie,* which appeared five years earlier. Nevertheless there is an increasing emphasis, as such descriptions pile up, on the way spontaneous sympathy and kinship are assets somehow more available to the impoverished than to anyone else in the book. This sentiment accumulates in the next to the last chapter when Lily, having taken her leave of Selden for what will prove the last time, sits in Bryant Park, a deserted and lonely figure. Again, what makes us feel the frailty and smallness of the heroine is the panoramic rendering of her surroundings. The park is located at the relatively unfashionable middle of Fifth Avenue, the most luxurious of the avenues in New York, a kind of gathering place for the unlocated, a passage from the private elegance of the East side to the public show places and tenements of the West. Discovered by Nettie Struther, one of the girls Lily has helped at Gerty's club for young women in distress, she goes to Nettie's apartment, to the warmth of her kitchen, and is there allowed to hold Nettie's newborn baby. In this scene, very nearly at the end of the book, Mrs. Wharton makes an anxious and contrived effort to evoke the kind of human relationship disastrously absent from Lily's life. She is suggesting some positive standard to which the reader and Lily might appeal for an alternative both to the community of dinginess, in which Lily feels condemned, and to the society in which she had hoped to live. It is a society, we now remember with some shock, in which there has been no evidence of children or of childbearing.

The most poignant moment in the scene shows Lily

holding Nettie's baby, and its poignancy is of a piece
with its metaphoric implications:

> The baby, feeling herself detached from her ha-
> bitual anchorage, made an instinctive motion
> of resistance; but the soothing influences of di-
> gestion prevailed, and Lily felt the soft weight
> sink trustfully against her breast. The child's
> confidence in its safety thrilled her with a sense
> of warmth and returning life, and she bent
> over, wondering at the rosy blur of the little
> face, the empty clearness of the eyes, the vague
> tendrilly motions of the folding and unfolding
> fingers. At first the burden in her arms seemed
> as light as a pink cloud or a heap of down, but
> as she continued to hold it the weight in-
> creased, sinking deeper, and penetrating her
> with a strange sense of weakness, as though the
> child entered into her and became a part of
> herself.

The passage is not making any simple-minded suggestion that Lily would have been happier had she been
satisfied with poverty and the common destiny of moth-
erhood. Directing our attention beyond the triviality of
such "solutions" is the metaphoric urgency of the passage, its efforts to grasp, like the "folding and unfolding
fingers" of the baby, an image of unity and natural kinship. Obvious enough in the last sentence, the intention
is implicit in the first: "The baby, feeling itself detached
from her habitual anchorage, made an instinctive motion of resistance." The metaphors remind us, by contrast, of the factitious social unities throughout the rest
of the novel, of alliances held together by the power of

money and by the shared hypocrisies that constitute a standard for the exclusion of Lily. She is soon to die alone in her bed with the drugged illusion that the baby is lying with her, "a gentle penetrating thrill of warmth and pleasure. She settled herself into an easier position, hollowing her arm to pillow the round downy head, and holding her breath lest a sound should disturb the sleeping child." Her tenderness, expending itself at the end on thin air, is an expression of the instinctive compassion that has led to her ruin.

In the society in which Lily has been living, there have not been nor could there be the spontaneous enactments of human solidarity that we witness among Lily, the baby, and Nettie. The contrast is impressed upon us with so little evidence of the author's conscious contrivance that it seems to come from her most inward feeling for her material. Thus we discover, looking back, that Lily's response to Mrs. Dorset and to her schemes was described in nearly the same terms used in the scene with the child: "But compassion, in a moment, got the better of her instinctive recoil from Mrs. Dorset," just as the baby after an "instinctive motion of resistance" surrenders to a desire for warmth and unity. And the metaphoric parallels are further evident in Lily's then thinking of herself as a motherly source of comfort even to her enemy: "it was on Lily's lips to exclaim: 'You poor soul, don't double and turn — come straight to me and we'll find a way out!'"

What is particularly interesting about this novel, and about some of the other works of American literature we have considered, is that the author cannot authenticate her sentiments about compassion and kinship; she cannot give them a positive embodiment in dramatic scenes without going outside the areas of society where the central conflicts of her work have occurred. Instead, she moves into areas tangential to them and occupied by characters mostly anonymous. One implication of the metaphors used to describe such characters is that their sympathy and their recognition of human destinies, other than merely social ones, can be a basis for kinship and community more binding than the power of money. It is here that Mrs. Wharton's admiration for George Eliot seems to have entered as a determining factor in *The House of Mirth*. Lily's sacrificial sympathy for Mrs. Dorset is much like Dorothea Brooke's in several comparable scenes, especially with Rosamond, at the end of *Middlemarch*.

George Eliot's treatment of personal relations is impassioned by her knowledge of the social fractures in English society that developed on the eve of the Reform Bill of 1832. Of the possible healing unities that are proposed in *Middlemarch*, the tragic inadequacy of the economic and especially the scientific schemes in which the novel abounds are obvious enough. The only dependable social unities that are achieved derive from a kind of Wordsworthean sympathy defined by Ladislaw in his description of a soul "in which knowledge passes instantaneously into feeling, and feeling flashes back as a new organ of knowledge." It is a measure of the difference between the historical situations of the English novelist in 1870 and of the American in 1905 that Mrs. Wharton does not imagine a society in which her heroine can do more than carry out the first part of Ladislaw's prescription. She transforms her knowledge into compassion. But her expression of compassion reveals an ignorance of the nature of her environment that could come only from a beautiful and uncynical nature. Characters like Mrs. Dorset are not motivated by needs and feelings that in George Eliot's moral universe are considered inherently human.

To assume such motivation in the people of *The House of Mirth* is to be admirably and simply a dupe, an innocent. In making Lily what we might call an old-fashioned American who believes that people remain as children in their need for love and sympathy, Mrs. Wharton is not herself in the least an innocent. She knows her heroine well enough to recognize that Lily's unsuspicious nature is in part an expression of ego, the underside of innocence: she has the capacity to think so well of herself that she cannot easily imagine the gross intentions of others with respect to her. Thus when Trenor demands payment of her debts to him he needs to instruct her in the fact that he is not "asking for payment in kind." Her affections will be a proper substitute for his money. All that saves Lily on this occasion is something remaining in Trenor of the social standards whose passing Mrs. Wharton laments in her autobiography. Trenor is prevented from forcing his attentions on Lily, we are told, when "old habits, old restraints, the hand of inherited order, plucked back the bewildered mind which passion had jolted from its ruts."

Even so short a quotation indicates that this moment is one of the weakest in the novel, both in its characterization and in the platitudinous coloration of style, not uncommon in the ladies' magazines for which Mrs. Wharton sometimes wrote. In the scene between Lily and Trenor, Mrs. Wharton tries, quite unsuccessfully I'm afraid, to unite the central areas of social drama in her novel with the standards by which she is most anxious to judge it, standards which she would like to believe are still, if weakly, operative in that society. Her failure at this moment perhaps dissuaded her from any further efforts of the same kind and made it necessary for her to locate analogous standards of human decency in areas uncontaminated by the social forces dominant in the book. At the end, Lily Bart's misery is said to have proceeded from her having been denied an ordering principle for her good impulses. She is without the benefit of those raised, like George Eliot's rural family the Garths, in a community united by memories and customs. "It was indeed miserable to be poor," Lily thinks just before her accidental suicide, and she continues:

> . . . to look forward to a shabby, anxious middleage, leading by dreary degrees of economy and self-denial to gradual absorption in the dingy communal existence of the boarding-house. But there was something more miserable still — it was the clutch of solitude at her heart, the sense of being swept like a stray uprooted growth down the heedless current of the years. That was the feeling which possessed her now — the feeling of being something rootless and ephemeral, mere spindrift of the whirling surface of existence, without anything to which the poor little tentacles of self could cling before the awful flood submerged them. And as she looked back she saw that there had never been a time when she had had any real relation to life. Her parents too had been rootless, blown hither and thither on every wind of fashion,

without any personal existence to shelter them
from its shifting gusts. She herself had grown
up without any one spot of earth being dearer
to her than another: there was no center of
early pieties, of grave endearing traditions, to
which her heart could revert and from which
it could draw strength for itself and tenderness
for others. In whatever form, a slowly-accumu-
lated past lives in the blood — whether in the
concrete image of the old house stored with
visual memories, or in a conception of the
house not built with hands but made up of inherited passions and loyalties — it has the same
power of broadening and deepening the individual existence, of attaching it by mysterious
links of kinship to all the mighty sum of human striving.

The assumptions in this paragraph are also George
Eliot's, whose conservatism is particularly admired by
Mrs. Wharton in her review of Leslie Stephen's *George
Eliot:* "a deep reverence for family ties, for the sancti-
ties of tradition, the claims of slowly acquired convic-
tions and slowly formed precedents, is revealed in every
page of her books." This particular kind of reverence
has since developed into the mythology of the anti-
urban and politically conservative literature of the twentieth century. Familiar to readers of Faulkner or Yeats
or T. S. Eliot's essays on culture, the mythology invests
heavily in Mrs. Wharton's vocabulary: "rootless," "one
spot of earth," "early pieties," "inherited passions and
loyalties," "traditions," and the mystique of the "house
not built by hands but made up of inherited passions

and loyalties." Mrs. Wharton's dream of environment is conspicuously different from any she can represent.

Her use of the vocabulary of "tradition" has the ring of platitude. The reason is by now perhaps obvious: the terms as used in *The House of Mirth* are given no nourishing connections to the dramatic substance of the novel. They have their source mostly in the episode of Lily's quite accidental meeting with Nettie Struther, who has not before had any place in the book. There is an air of extemporization precisely at the point where Mrs. Wharton is trying to give us something to carry away, other than a helpless sense of pity and revulsion, from the disasters we have witnessed. What she can give us is merely a vocabulary. Sharing George Eliot's attitude, she is deprived of George Eliot's resources — a society in which there really were "grave and endearing traditions" still in visible and audible form. And because she is a novelist who could not create such a society in her language, she is the more evidently a victim herself of social forces that also defeat her heroine.

Some of the contradictions among critics assessing the illusive role of Selden in this novel result from not fully grasping the literary significance of Mrs. Wharton's dedication to rural traditionalism. Selden has all the intellectual refinements that allows him "a happy air of viewing the show objectively, of having points of contact outside the great gilt cage." But his "points of contact" are essentially to literary and philosophical abstractions and exclude the kinds of contact fatally missing from Lily's life. His "republic of the spirit" is not Mrs. Wharton's ideal community. He is allowed to catch Lily in situations compromising enough to make most men cautious, though not the kind of man Mrs.

Wharton characteristically admired in her novels. Selden's feelings are often as calculated as those coming
from inside "the great gilt cage." He too judges Lily
more by conventional assumptions of propriety than by
knowing and trusting her through his affections. When
she is most in need of him, after Mrs. Dorset, in a brilliantly paced scene of social tension, forbids her to return to the yacht, Selden offers her everything but the
support of his trust: "The memory of Mrs. Fisher's
hints, and the corroboration of his own impressions,
while they deepened his pity, also increased his con-
straint, since, whichever way he sought a free outlet for
sympathy, it was blocked by the fear of committing a
blunder." He is afraid of precisely those impulses by
which Lily continually and sympathetically responds to
Mrs. Dorset, with whom Selden has had assignations.
These alone make it clear that Mrs. Wharton is not giving us a portrait of masculine sexual incapacity. Selden's
somewhat murky characterization is instead a result of
her not having found a way, especially at the early stages
of the book, to make about him the point that we can
make only retrospectively, looking back from the meeting of Lily and Nettie: that he is deficient in a sense of
human solidarity and that he knows others not by loving but only by judging them.

The characterization of Selden is an instance of Mrs.
Wharton's difficulty in having her standards emanate
from within the conflicts she is dramatizing. He is refined, intelligent, and courageously self-consulting within a rigidly conformist environment, but his ways of
"knowing" people are essentially cosmopolitan — by the
guesswork, the gossip, the categorizing assumptions that
substitute for the slowly accumulated intimacy on which

Mrs. Wharton places such redeeming value. He is unable, by character and circumstance, to "know" Lily as people of George Eliot's provincial *Middlemarch* can at their best know one another or as Faulkner's characters can know, for example, that one of their number did not commit a crime even though all the apparent evidence indicates that he did. Again, the character in this novel who exercises this kind of knowledge has no place whatever in the major line of action. He belongs instead to Nettie's story, which might be called a pastoral version of Lily's: she became unfortunately involved with a "stylish" man, was left ill and disgraced by him until rescued (with the help of some money from Lily) by Gerty, who is also ready to assist Lily in her distress.

But the difference in Nettie's story, and it has made all the difference, is a character named George. He has known her since childhood and thus with an intimacy that can make him compassionate rather than critical of her later behavior. The vocabulary which Mrs. Wharton gives Nettie confirms once again the relevance to this novel of George Eliot. George Eliot provides the classic image in fiction of a kind of social communion derived, as in later anti-cosmopolitan fiction, from "some center of early pieties . . . of grave endearing traditions to which the heart could revert and from which it could draw strength for itself and tenderness for others." Nettie ends her story with the happy news that "when I got back home, George came round and asked me to marry him. At first I thought I couldn't, because we'd been brought up together, and I knew he knew about me. But after awhile I began to see that that made it easier. I never could have told another man, and I'd never have married without telling; but if George cared enough to have me as I was, I didn't see why I shouldn't begin again — and I did."

"And I knew he knew about me" — this compassionate use of knowledge allows us to measure the failure of Selden in his treatment of Lily. He is, we were told earlier, unable to "yield to the growth of an affection which might appeal to pity yet leave the understanding untouched: sympathy would no more delude him than a trick of the eyes, the grace of helplessness than a curve of the cheek." The tone here is partisanly feminine in the suggestion, not sustained by the characterization of Selden in his relationships with women, that he is a sexually unimpassioned man. Here again the basis for some of Mrs. Wharton's attitudes fails to be sufficiently objectified within the fictional world she creates. The trouble with Selden is that he will not allow himself to "know" the heroine through his instincts, his spontaneous affections.

But who *can* know her? Beyond Selden there is only the rhetoric which praises the conditions within which a good way of knowing her might have been fostered by the "grave endearing traditions" not available to anyone except, in some apparently elementary form, to Nettie and her George and to the pitiable Gerty. Mrs. Wharton's difficulty in *The House of Mirth* makes any comparison to the English women novelists with whom she deserves to keep company end with a significant degree of contrast. She is a novelist of manners in a peculiarly American way: she cannot imagine a society, any more than can Emerson or most of the other writers I have considered, in which her values are brought into play at the center of dramatic conflict. Instead of being an aggregate of human relationships, subject to modification in the best interest of its members, society for her as for a majority of American writers becomes an expression of impersonal power, even when that power is being manipulated by some of its victims.

### III

Nine years younger than Edith Wharton, and ages behind her in literary and social sophistication, Dreiser wrote *Sister Carrie* out of an instinctive awareness of what Mrs. Wharton would later propose in *The House of Mirth:* that society is composed not of personal relationships extended into historical and communal ones, but that it is made up of forces to which these relationships are irrelevant. At the end of the earlier work, Carrie Meeber, even with the success Lily fails to get, gazes no less yearningly at the same panorama of glittering power: from her chambers at the Waldorf she looks "out upon the old winding procession of carriages rolling up Fifth Avenue." After Carrie's success no less than during Lily's failure there persists what Dreiser calls the never satisfied "strivings of the human heart."

Dreiser belongs "in a very old, a very difficult, a very lonely American tradition," where Alfred Kazin has placed him: "It is no longer 'transcendentalist' but always it seeks to transcend," Kazin writes . . . "he does not accept our 'society' as the whole of reality." And he refuses to see very much reality at all in those early pieties, endearing traditions, and family ties promoted by Mrs. Wharton, however ineffectively, as a possible amelioration to the disastrous failures of her heroines. Dreiser's indifference to the saving grace of personal relationships cannot be explained as a deficiency of imagi-

nation or experience, though to have any of either
means that you do not have all. There was, in fact,
considerable warmth within his large, mobile, impoverished family. His father was cold and religiously austere,
but Theodore and his brother Paul formed a lifelong
attachment and when Dreiser thought of their mother,
in *A Book About Myself,* it was of "a magnetic dreamy
soul . . . beyond or behind so-called good or evil," a
woman without much "constructive ability wherewith
to make real her dreams." Similarly, it only partly explains his lack of interest in the novelistic intensities of
personal relationships to say that he was ignorant of the
literary conventions that had endowed them with
mythic and symbolic importance. "The costly price of
sons and lovers," Emerson called such relationships in
"Experience," remarking that he would gladly pay the
price *if* this would "introduce me into . . . reality."
Reality for Emerson, though associated with different
forces than for Dreiser, is even more infinitely beyond
the measure of merely personal fates.

Dreiser was infatuated primarily by the movements,
more often the mere "driftings" of single persons within
huge dimensions of impersonal force. Environment in
his work becomes synonymous not only with the City as
mass but with life itself as energy, the latter phenomenon being especially evident in his later works. He
exults, like an awed discoverer of regions where he will
probably himself be destroyed, in mapping those forces
against which, first in George Eliot, then in Hardy, then
in Lawrence, human relatedness of a kind nearly ignored by Dreiser offers the only hope of a personal, as
distinguished from an anonymous existence.

Stuart Sherman did not know how right he was fifteen

years after *Sister Carrie,* and nearly coincident with the
publication of *The "Genius,"* when he announced in
"The Barbaric Naturalism of Theodore Dreiser" that
"Mr. Dreiser's field seems curiously outside American
society." For Sherman, as for Gertrude Atherton, who
said of Dreiser's characters that "not a real American
could be found among them with a magnifying glass,"
American society was a sort of Anglo-Saxon literary club.
Necessarily on the outside of this, a product, Sherman
was not beneath observing, of the German element of
our "mixed population," Dreiser portrayed a "vacuum,
from which the obligations of parenthood, marriage,
chivalry, and citizenship have been quite withdrawn."
The triviality of the judgment is sufficiently indicated by
pointing out that the "vacuum" thus described was also
created by a writer as impeccably Anglo-Saxon as Emerson when, in the woods, he discovered that "the name of
the nearest friend sounds then foreign and accidental:
to be brothers, to be acquaintances, master or servant, is
then a trifle and a disturbance."

To be "outside American society" is of course to be in
the great American literary tradition. It is a tradition,
transcendentalism and romanticism being only two aspects of it, in which individuals are characterized less by
their relation to one another than by their relation to
the conglomerations of power that fill space and that determine the apportionments of time. The conglomerations go under different names: Nature, The City,
Society, The Dynamo, The Bomb, The Presidency, and
aspects of any one of these may be ascribed to any other.
The force that joins people together in Dreiser's world
does not manifest itself in marriage, any more than it
does in most other American writers. People are instead

merged in a common bondage to the humming, souring vistas of the city with their evocations of mysterious promise. Personal attachments, sporadic and "chemic," can take place within such an environment, but they do not compel the interest of Dreiser or his characters. These characters are compelled instead by the non-personal forces that fill the yearning eye with steel and concrete, that manipulate time by the pulsations of manufacture and of money-making.

The time and space of a novel like *Sister Carrie,* or of most of his other novels, is, by comparison to what is given to personal relations, inordinately devoted to the panorama of the City. There is nothing therefore surprising in the way the novel was begun. After exchanging promises with Arthur Henry, with whom Dreiser had worked on the *Toledo Blade,* that they would both write novels, Dreiser merely sat down and put the words of his title at the top of a page without any idea how he was to fill it or succeeding ones. "My mind was a blank," he tells us in *A Book About Myself,* "except for the name. I had no idea who or what she was to be. I have often thought there was something mystic about it, as if I were being used, like a medium." The two words, the blank page, soon to be filled, are symptomatic that so far as character and environment are concerned Dreiser had no intention of creating anything like a Jamesian "house of fiction." The shape of the material was the shape for the most part merely of his recollections. Writing for him obviously did not involve the "building" of a world so much as reporting on one already existent. In fact, the career of Carrie Meeber is in many ways a report of the experience of one of Dreiser's sisters. About the only pattern of disruption in the sequence of reported lives occurs when Dreiser

wants to place different kinds of environment in juxtaposition, as when the squalor of the factory where
Carrie works is contrasted with the elegance of Fitzgerald
and Moy's where the men discuss her. Characteristically,
where there is most evidence of concern for presentation, for premeditated organization, there is less care
given to the characterization of Carrie than to her
environmental situations. It is as if she herself were only
part of that environment, a mostly silent figure within
the massed, detailed, panoramic globs of language that
create it. Environmental force is made altogether more
articulate than are any of the characters in the book.

This inarticulateness of persons extends almost as
poignantly to Dreiser himself. It is implicit even in his
volubility. The floods of language by which he embraces
things outside himself are a verbal equivalent to the visual obsessions of his characters. Not until at least his
third novel, *The Financier* in 1912, could one sometimes
hear in this volubility anything like a firm or authoritative presence of Dreiser himself. In *Sister Carrie* it is
impossible to discover him except in disparate frag-
ments. As much as does his heroine or Hurstwood,
Dreiser becomes lost to the evoked environments of the
book. To reach any assessment of his historical significance as a writer, a question has to be asked this early in
his career: who *is* Theodore Dreiser in these pages? At
issue is not the fact that he is a different "sounding" person from one page to another. Such transformations are
a virtue in most writers and in most people. What is
perplexing is that he creates no plastic coherence among
the lurid varieties of self-characterization that emerge
from his language. His relationship to the reader and to
his material is fragmented. His flaccid poetizing, his
fatalistic jowl-shaking about sexual compulsions, his

verbal endorsements of meretricious glamor side by side with portentously critical assessments of it — the failure of attention to the composite results of these various tones raises questions not answered by the usual attacks on the slovenliness of his style. Granted that he often writes as if language itself were a bore, there remains the mystery of Dreiser's undeniable power over the imagination even of his severest critics.

In one sense, the fractured characterization which Dreiser gives to himself as narrator of *Sister Carrie* is evidence of the integrity of his vision. It is a vision in which character — as a derivative of language and the power of language — is regarded as relatively negligible. In his apparent reluctance to cope with his own fluctuations of voice, Dreiser is in no way protecting himself. Instead, and to an extraordinary degree, he seems not even to care about achieving through language any shaped social identity. To care about doing so would be a concession to the idea, on which most English novels are based, that persons and societies are literally "made" by personal exertion or by the ability to give authoritative shapes to words. Indeed what I find admirable in Dreiser is that he does not in any way compromise himself by subscribing to a bourgeois faith in the reality of language. His essentially religious energy, his personal necessity would not let him adulterate his vision of environment as comprised of chemic, economic, and natural force. He simply cannot permit, for the sake of story or of "literature," those conversational involvements that imply that the self or society is formed by intensities of personal effort. For him, character and society are antecedent to talk; fate has nothing to do with the value of certain words and phrases, with the conflict between people or between a person and his environment.

Correspondingly, the language used by his characters has relatively little to do with creating or sustaining their personal relationships: in their conversations they merely report to each other how external forces are combining or separating their human destinies. Naturally, he is more effective when writing scenes of separation than of meeting, scenes where people can no longer talk rather than scenes where they must talk out of a compulsion of initial attraction. Three such very effective moments reveal Carrie's progress, partly because the breakup, like the formation of relations in Dreiser, is in obedience to accelerations of success or failure. When she leaves her sister and brother-in-law to escape from Wabash Avenue to the "elegance" of life with Drouet she merely absents herself after dinner. She goes into the bathroom, where they cannot disturb her, and writes a little note:

> "Good-bye, Minnie," it read. "I'm not going home. I'm going to stay in Chicago a little while and look for work. Don't worry. I'll be all right."
>
> In the front room Hanson was reading his paper. As usual, she helped Minnie clear away the dishes and straighten up. Then she said:
>
> "I guess I'll stand down at the door a little while." She could scarcely prevent her voice from trembling.
>
> Minnie remembered Hanson's remonstrance.

"Sven doesn't think it looks good to stand down there," she said.

"Doesn't he?" said Carrie. "I won't do it any more after this."

She put on her hat and fidgeted around the table in the little bedroom, wondering where to slip the note. Finally she put it under Minnie's hair-brush.

When she had closed the hall-door, she paused a moment and wondered what they would think. Some thought of the queerness of her deed affected her. She went slowly down the stairs. She looked back up the lighted step, and then affected to stroll up the street. When she reached the corner she quickened her pace.

As she was hurrying away, Hanson came back to his wife.

"Is Carrie down at the door again?" he asked.

"Yes," said Minnie; "she said she wasn't going to do it any more."

He went over to the baby where it was playing on the floor and began to poke his finger at it.

Drouet was on the corner waiting, in good spirits.

"Hello, Carrie," he said, as a sprightly figure of a girl drew near him. "Got here safe, did you? Well, we'll take a car."

She will subsequently leave Drouet for Hurstwood with only slightly more ceremony, occasioned by Drouet's wish that she should stay, and still later, also in the interests of her career, she will leave Hurstwood in a scene not significantly different from the one just quoted. Hurstwood returns to find a note in Carrie's inimitably simple, unapologetic style:

> "Dear George," he read, crunching the money in one hand. "I'm going away. I'm not coming back any more. It's no use trying to keep up the flat; I can't do it. I wouldn't mind helping you, if I could, but I can't support us both, and pay the rent. I need what little I make to pay for my clothes. I'm leaving twenty dollars. It's all I have just now. You can do whatever you like with the furniture. I won't want it. — Carrie."

He dropped the note and looked quietly round. Now he knew what he missed. It was the little ornamental clock, which was hers. It had gone from the mantelpiece. He went into the front room, his bedroom, the parlour, lighting the gas as he went. From the chiffoniere had gone the knick-nacks of silver and plate. From the table-top, the lace coverings. He opened the wardrobe — no clothes of hers. He opened the drawers — nothing of hers. Her trunk was gone from its accustomed place. Back in his own room hung his old clothes, just as he had left them. Nothing else was gone.

He stepped into the parlour and stood for a few moments looking vacantly at the floor. The silence grew oppressive. The little flat seemed wonderfully deserted. He wholly for-

got that he was hungry, that it was only din-
ner-time. It seemed later in the night.

Suddenly, he found that the money was still
in his hands. There were twenty dollars in all,
as she had said. Now he walked back, leaving
the lights ablaze, and feeling as if the flat were
empty.

"I'll get out of this," he said to himself.

Then the sheer loneliness of his situation
rushed upon him in full.

"Left me!" he muttered and repeated, "Left
me!"

The place that had been so comfortable,
where he had spent so many days of warmth,
was now a memory. Something colder and chill-
ier confronted him. He sank down in his
chair, resting his chin in his hands — mere sen-
sation, without thought, holding him.

Then something like a bereaved affection
and self pity swept over him.

"She needn't have gone away," he said. "I'd
have got something."

He sat a long while without rocking, and
added quite clearly, out loud: "I tried, didn't
I?"

At midnight he was still rocking, staring at
the floor.

The circumstances in each of these scenes are, conventionally, among the most dramatically exploitable in
literature: the rejection of family, the casting off of one
lover and the taking of another, the final collapse of the
central relationship of the book and of the heroine. But

in each instance Dreiser disdains his dramatic opportunity. No direct confrontation, with its inherent possibilities of conversational drama, is allowed to take place between his people. Instead, his characters reveal their feelings in a manner — notes of departure, soliloquies, primitive interior monologue, all of these in the simplest grammatical structure — that expresses the impossibility or, perhaps one should say, the lack of necessity for dialogue.

The clue to the significance of this pattern is, I think, in the fact that what moves Carrie in each episode, and what therefore moves the plot, is sexual impulse. More accurately, Carrie discovers that her sexual interests are excited by the economic and social power in the men she meets. In his novels, no less than in his autobiographical writing, Dreiser was determined that sex should be recognized as "the controlling and directing force that it is." The distinction which Leslie Stephen made between Fielding and Richardson, letting Fielding represent the truly masculine and Richardson the more feminine way of treating sex, could as easily describe the difference between Dreiser and most American novelists before him. Sexuality, firm and insistent in its pressure, is what ultimately gets communicated by these scenes; the inarticulateness of his characters and yet their strange, indeflectable movement toward or away from one another, even when they are in most respects conspicuously "drifting," gives us the image of truly seduced persons. It was perhaps in reference to this phenomenon that Randolph Bourne, in his review of *The 'Genius,'* observed that Dreiser's "hero is really not Sister Carrie or the Titan or the Genius, but that desire within us that pounds in manifold guise against the iron

walls of experience." The "iron walls of experience"
might well remind us of Hawthorne's "iron fetters we
call reality" though it is here sexual impulse that
"pounds against" rather than the "imagination" that
merely "lessens" the oppressive surroundings. It is as if
sex in Dreiser were almost the only imaginable form of
personal interchange since all other contacts have been
reduced to the account characters might give of their
daily schedules.

Nevertheless, sex in Dreiser does not enrich relationships beyond what they initially were. Sex is merely the
instrument of a compulsion to have a relationship, a
compulsion excited by a whole complex of inarticulate
excitations about the representative glamor of a particular person. Of some autobiographical relevance is
Dreiser's admission that he found it "almost affectionately unavoidable to hold three, four — even as many
as five and six — women in regard — at one and the same
time." His compulsion (and his good luck at escaping its
consequences) was the result perhaps of sterility. But on
the evidence of his novels he was in any case someone
not aware of the emotional responsibilities and convolu-
tions, the whole element of "play" in human relationships which are the mainstay of other novelists. At the
end of what in most novels would be very complicated
human attachments, his characters simply walk off.

This curious, this very sad and touching sequence by
which his people are dispersed into the landscape of the
City places Dreiser within that line of American writers
who choose not to imagine what I have earlier called a
society of alternatives. At the end of *Sister Carrie* nothing has been accumulated from the tangled relationships which hold any two people together, nothing of a
personal kind modifies their distress at being in a re-

lationship merely to external force. The novel's last pages, a sort of passing in review of the characters each going his separate way, provide images not so much of isolation as of persons meaningfully related only to the scenery of urban energy or, in Hurstwood's case, indifferently destined for death soon after leaving the anonymous band of brothers auctioned off in the Bowery for money to pay for their beds.

Dreiser's literary characteristics make it predictable that in 1934 he would write an essay called "The Myth of Individuality." He there develops the idea that "man is not living, but is being lived by something which needs not only him but billions like him in order to express itself." There is no contradiction in turning, as he did, from a concept of mechanism to a concept of totality, to what he called "Universe, God, or the Vital Force," quoting in the process Emerson's "Brahma." And Thoreau, he admitted, was of all the philosophers he read the "most illuminative . . . of a universal and apparently beneficient control . . . however dark and savage its results or expressions may seem to us at times." Matthiessen, who gives a good account of this development, errs, I think, in remarking that Dreiser's discovery of kinship with "such a highly individualistic philosopher fills out the bases of his political beliefs in a way that his hurried pamphleteering often failed to do. He had arrived at the conviction that man cannot find fulfillment except through society. But he had not lost the individual in the mass. . . ."

Insofar as society existed at all for Dreiser, however, it was as impossibly visionary as any imagined by Thoreau. Thoreau's most ecstatic image of "society" comes at the end of *Walden*. It is of men individually disjointed so that they might then join — a nose here, a

liver there — in a formative process which is the excrementitious flow of Nature, from which emerges
"the world and me." Emerson and Thoreau do share
with Dreiser a concept of "individuality." But "individuality" for them is quite unrecognizable in Matthiessen's or in the ordinary use of the term. In their works,
"individuality" does of course refer to non-conformism,
social protest, and a sense of human destiny not satisfied
by the opportunities available within the structure of
society. Self-affirmation of this sort is only a prelude,
however, to a quite different, altogether more "eccentric" kind of individuality wherein Dreiser, Emerson,
and Thoreau begin to show important affinities. This is
the "individuality" achieved by the surrender of those
features which define the individual as a social or psychological entity. "Individuality" becomes indistinguishable, from a social point of view — the point of view
of most novelists, let us say — from anonymity. What
happens to a man's body or his voice in the Over-Soul
or within the movements of Thoreau's Nature is scarcely
distinguishable from what happens to him when, in Dreiser, he is "being lived by something which needs not only
him but billions like him in order to express itself."

The horror of this formulation ("billions like him")
is alleviated only in part by the fact that the "something" to which Dreiser refers is so vague as to be politically harmless, "something" half cosmic, half socialistic.
The notion of individuality operative in his works does
have a political career and, I would suspect, a predictable one. The fact that Dreiser's Emersonianism had to
locate itself in spaces actually filled not by the spirit of
Nature but by the spirit of the City, the spirit of the
mass yearning for what finance capitalism promised to

give it, partly explains his decision to join the Communist Party as a symbolic act of what he liked to think of as "international" solidarity. One reason his novels are of interest now, I think, is for the speculation they excite about the possible connections between his kind of literary imagination (what Lionel Trilling has called the liberal imagination) and political inclinations to the Left, much as in the very different imaginations of Eliot, Pound, or Wyndham Lewis we catch their leanings — or fallings — in the opposite political direction. I am not talking about the political bases for the critical reception of Dreiser, but about the political analogues to the very way in which his novels project reality. Not surprisingly, Dreiser is seldom even considered a "modern" writer· he had no interest in individual consciousness, in personal complexity, in those traditional and communal feelings which, according to the pseudo-medical testimony of certain people, run in their blood streams. He had no truck with personal, cultural, or literary "organicism," no concern, finally, even with the absence of an "organic society." These are among the *raison d'être* for the stylistic difficulties of "modern" literature and for the corresponding development of these formal criteria which have dissuaded readers from looking enough at Dreiser to see that he belongs in the strongest tradition of American literature and that in his blatant strangeness he redefines some filaments of that tradition for us.

That creative and shaping force which earlier American writers found in Nature or in the composite man called the Poet is located by Dreiser in the objects that fill what were the free spaces of America. Encoded for him in the artifacts we have produced is not the power of

individual men — who, after all, *did* build or even
dream the skyline of New York? — but of what Dreiser
calls "mass ideals." "I wish to make it perfectly clear,"
he writes in "The Essential Tragedy of Life," "that I
am by no means confusing the race with the individual,
or vice versa. What a race may do, and what man may,
are two very different things. The race, representing the
totality of active creations and pushed on by dynamic
forces from below, may be, and in so far as one can guess
is, a huge success." Dreiser's cataloguing of the visible
evidences of this "dynamic force" is in a voice that continually loses its individual authority, and I in no way
intend this as a criticism. Like other admirers of Dreiser,
I am compelled by the very fluctuations and unsteadi-
ness of his voice, revealing as it does the extraordinary
degree to which he can be intimidated by the Things he
describes, even by the banalities of conversation he reports: "There is a world of accumulated feeling back of
the trite dramatic expression," he assures us. Anything
for Dreiser, a skyscraper or a shop window, is part of the
hieroglyph of "the race." It is nagging to ask that in
the face of this there should be in his style anything like
a firmly consistent individual presence.

Concluding this book with Dreiser, there is of course
a temptation to find in him some culmination of the
issues I have raised about self and environment or to
treat him as a historical-literary link between the nineteenth and twentieth centuries. But in its emphasis on
the dialectical struggle over these issues in the style of individual works and on the similarities proposed between
writers separated by more than a century, as are Emerson
and Fitzgerald, this book has denied itself the benefits
of culmination or prediction. We can look forward
from the Dreiser who in *Sister Carrie* hears "The voice

of the so-called inanimate!" to the comic-apocalyptic writers of the present decade, where, as in the works of Thomas Pynchon, human beings drift into the category of the inanimate. But having done so, we are cheated of progression by reminders from R. W. B. Lewis that we can look back from them to Melville. Melville's Ishmael also finds the essence of man buried under accumulations of history, and he takes a quite darker view than does Dreiser of what this accumulation tells us about the race:

> Winding far down from within the very heart of this spiked Hotel de Cluny where we here stand — however grand and wonderful, now quit it; — and take your way, ye nobler, sadder souls, to those vast Roman halls of Thermes; where far beneath the fantastic towers of man's upper earth, his root of grandeur, his whole awful essence sits in bearded state; an antique buried beneath antiquities, and throned on torsoes! So with a broken throne, the great gods mock that captive king; so like a Caryatid, he patient sits, upholding on his frozen brow the piled entabulatures of ages. Wind ye down there, ye prouder, sadder souls!

As Charles Feidelson points out, the passage suggests that the lost potentialities of man are smothered under accretions of the ages, under what Melville calls, in an image Dreiser himself might have used, "the fantastic towers of man's upper earth." Radically unlike one another as they are, *Moby-Dick* and the works of Dreiser are in some sense about their own voracious accumulations of material, about, in Melville's case, a vast allusiveness to the literary, technological, philosphical authorities that cripple the free articulation of individual consciousness. Of *Moby-Dick* the book as of Moby-Dick the whale, Ahab might cry that it "heaps me."

It may be that as a historical and scientific development the power evoked by Dreiser and described by Henry Adams now feeds at an accelerated rate on its own creations. It may be, too, that human consciousness, failing to develop at a pace with the technology it has created, is to be reduced to the muteness of Dreiser's characters or to the monomania of Melville's. But American literature chose to confront this horror, in Cooper's *The Crater* as well as in *Moby-Dick,* before history verified it. And it continues to confront it after the verifications. These more recent confrontations are if anything less grim than the earlier ones. In Faulkner and Fitzgerald, in Nabokov and Mailer is a resurgence of the Emersonian dream of possibly "building" a world out of the self in a style that is that self. The effort in *Lolita* to preserve an "intangible island of entranced time" succeeds no more than did the efforts in *The Crater,* over a hundred years before, to preserve an island paradise from the contaminations of modern democratic America. But such efforts are celebrated by these and by the other American writers perhaps because success *is* forbidden them by realities other than style, by exigencies of time and space. The effort is celebrated because even out of the perverse design of Nabokov's hero there emerges those marvels of human ingenuity, those exuberances of imagination, those extravagances of yearning that create the objects they yearn for — these are the evidences still in American literature of the continuing struggle of consciousness toward some further created being and some other world.

# Index of Authors

# Index of Works

255